REBORN IN THE WEST

REBORN IN THE WEST

The Reincarnation Masters

Vicki Mackenzie

BLOOMSBURY

First published in Great Britain in 1995

Bloomsbury Publishing Plc, 2 Soho Square, London W1V 5DE

PICTURE SOURCES

Vicki Mackenzie: page 1 *top*
Courtesy of Tenzin Sherab: page 1 *bottom* and 2 *top*
Courtesy of KPC: page 2 *bottom*
Andrew Doust: pages 3 and 4
Courtesy of FPMT: page 5
Basili Llorca: page 6 *bottom*
Courtesy of Jan Nichols: page 7 *top*
Courtesy of Namgyal: page 7 *bottom left*
Courtesy of Instituto Lama Tsong Khapa: page 7 *bottom right*
Roger Kunsang: page 8 *top left*
Fran Mahoupt: page 8 *top right*
Robin Bath: page 8 *bottom*

A CIP catalogue record for this book is
available from the British Library

ISBN 07475 1878 5

10 9 8 7 6 5 4 3 2 1

Typeset by Hewer Text Composition Services, Edinburgh
Printed in Great Britain by Clays Ltd, St Ives plc

For Andrew

My body like a water bubble
Decays and dies so very quickly
After death come results of Karma
Just like a shadow following a body

Lama Tsong Khapa
Fourteenth-century Tibetan scholar and mystic

CONTENTS

1

THE FIRST STEP

My journey into reincarnation began back in December 1976 when some inexplicable inner call led me to a hilltop called Kopan, in the middle of the Kathmandu valley, for a month-long meditation course run by two Tibetan lamas. To this day I still do not know precisely what prompted me to attempt such a thing, since at the time I had no knowledge of either meditation or Buddhism. But when a friend called me one day as I was sitting at my typewriter amid the general chaos of the *Daily Mail*, where I worked as a feature writer, and told me about her plan 'to meditate with the lamas', suddenly nothing seemed more alluring than to join her. There are rare times in your life when you not only hear the inner voice of intuition, but heed it. This was one of those moments, and it was a decision I was never to regret.

And so for twenty-eight days non-stop I immersed myself in an entirely different world. By night I slept in my sleeping bag on the floor in a funny little room where the icy winter blasts blew straight through the glassless windows. By day I steeped myself in the incomparable beauty of the Kopan Hill with its brightly coloured birds, its exotic, sweet-scented flowers, the view of the mighty Himalayan ranges and the ancient teachings of the Buddha. These were delivered by two of the most extraordinary human beings I had ever met. Lama Thubten Yeshe was the extrovert of the pair: round, warm, funny, at times outrageous, at times exquisitely touching, and always reaching out to us using whatever method he could to get his message across. Lama Zopa was his 'heart disciple', younger, introverted, ascetic, serious, with an air of unmistakable purity. Together they emanated all that I had ever thought spiritual beings should be. They were wise beyond measure, their wisdom springing not from bookish learning or dogmatic faith but from some deep well of inner experience. This was coupled with a radiating compassion, a sincere humility, and the most appealing characteristic of all, a well-developed sense of humour. I might not have bought *all* that they told me, for I am not by nature or training an easy believer, but I certainly bought them. If their religion had brought them to this point of human development, I argued, then it was worth staying around to hear what they had to say.

So, under the tin roof of the meditation hall, with the crows hopping about above, and the dogs barking in the valley below, I learned many things, including Tibetan Buddhism's answer to those biggest questions of all – the ones that have teased humankind through the ages: Who am I? Why am I here? Where did I come from? Where am I going to?

Later, when I was asked to write this book on reincarnation, I recalled the things the Lamas had said. For in the plethora of mounting material about past lives that presently surrounds us and our current fascination with it, no explanation has been so thoroughly defined, so systematically tried and tested as that offered by Tibetan Buddhism. The lamas had developed the mysteries that lay behind reincarnation to a precise science. Their wisdom was invaluable. What, after all, is the *point* of discovering you've been Toulouse-Lautrec or a poor serving wench in a past life? Entertainment value aside, the thinking person finally has to ask: 'So what?' The lamas had answers. They were complex, compelling and intellectually challenging.

They told us that we did not begin with our present life but that we had had many many lives before, stretching back to 'beginningless time'. It was a concept to tantalize the imagination. Furthermore, we would have many, many lives in the future. We circled round and round on the continuously revolving wheel of birth, ageing, sickness and death, they said, tossed hither and thither by our 'karma', that implacable law of cause and effect which dictates that what we sow so we shall reap. And so we go from lifetime to lifetime, learning our particular spiritual lessons, paying back karmic debts, reaping the results of all that we have done in the past, and all the while creating the conditions for our future rebirths.

It was all to do with the mind, our consciousness, they said, which in itself had no beginning and no end but existed in a continuous stream of awareness changing from moment to moment. Now mind, they told us, is not to be confused with the brain. They were quite definite. Consciousness, by definition, they said, has no physical properties; it is not made of matter and so cannot possibly be the same thing as that very fleshy organ filled with grey matter inside our heads. There is a connection, of course, they said, a strong connection, in the same way that electricity is connected to a light bulb, but it is definitely not synonymous. In fact the seat of our mind, they said, thumping their chests and beaming their warm, wise smiles, lies within our hearts.

I listened intrigued. Later I learned that Tibetan Buddhism's study of the mind was so profound and intimate that its lexicon contained some sixty words to depict its various meanings – rather like Eskimos have for snow. To fully comprehend it one had to study for at least thirty years to become a 'geshe' (the equivalent of a doctor of theology) and spend years in meditation, penetrating the meaning of consciousness for yourself. It was no wonder that the lamas were so exact, so sure in their explanations. Their words hit us with the full force of authenticity.

The crux of the whole issue of reincarnation, they continued, revolved around what happens at death. When we die, they said, our mind separates from our body and moves to its next existence taking on another form, another life. One had to admit that their reasoning at least was logical.

After years of regular churchgoing as a young person this was the closest definition of a soul that I had ever heard. Here was no woolly explanation like the response I had inevitably received when asking priests about what exactly a soul was. The lamas had managed to define that most elusive item of all and apparently had learnt how to work with it. Refining and developing our minds, they told us, was the most worthwhile thing a human being could do with his or her life, because ultimately it was all that we were left with.

If the theory sounded intellectual, the ramifications were not. This was about us and our lives – the ones we had now, the ones we had had in the past and the ones we were going to have in the future. The words the lamas spoke kept us all enthralled. The kind of existences we found ourselves in, they told us, were completely of our own making.

Basically the Buddhist law was simple. Positive actions lead to positive results, negative actions to negative results. Good, wholesome deeds of body, speech and mind, such as kindness, love, patience and generosity, brought forth happiness, while unwholesome acts such as anger, hatred, slander, jealousy and meanness came back in ways that would make us unhappy.

Long arguments and questions followed. The doctrine of karma may have been as old as ancient history itself, but to Westerners of the late twentieth century sitting on Kopan Hill these were revolutionary words indeed. For what the lamas were telling us in effect flew straight in the face of modern psychology. According to Buddhism it is not our mother or father, our upbringing, the government, the social system or our education which makes us what we are and causes our life situation, but us. We are the authors of our own lives, they said, past, present and future. What about genetics and heredity, I asked – those qualities and predispositions and illnesses which science has now proved come from our parents. 'Karma,' they replied, 'it's all karma. You choose your parents through the power of karma. Genetics and inheritance are, like everything else, controlled by the law of cause and effect.' They had answers for everything.

But what was the meaning of it all – this constant travelling from lifetime to lifetime with all its attendant experiences, good and bad? What was the point of continuously having to be born, only to die? Contemplating the prospect of the number of lives I could have had since 'beginningless time' was thoroughly exhausting. It was at this point that the lamas announced that there was an end to all this journeying. It is the destiny of each and every one of us, they said, to get off the wheel of life and death, to come to a place of perpetual rest and peace; for each and every one of us has the seed of Buddha nature within. Our Buddha nature, they explained, is consciousness developed to its highest point. It is the fully awakened mind, which knows all things and is characterized by a state of perpetual peace. It sounded good.

All we had to do to achieve it, they said, was to eliminate karma, and to achieve *that* we had to eliminate our delusions. Our delusions were like clouds that covered our enlightened state. There were, they said, umpteen delusions – faulty ways of thinking and behaving. But the biggest one of all, the one that caused all the trouble, was our primordial ignorance that stopped us seeing things as they really were. Fix ignorance, they said, and you fix the lot.

It was all rich food for thought. More questions and arguments ensued. The lamas loved it. They had been brought up on debate, which they maintained was *the* way of learning. Besides, the Buddha himself had decreed that no one should accept his teachings on blind faith but should test his words personally to find the truth for him or herself. 'You check up, check up!' exhorted the irrepressible Lama Yeshe.

The lamas had done their own 'checking up', and furthermore had evidence that what they were saying was true. They knew of countless spiritual adepts in Tibet, they told us, who through the ages had demonstrated their mastery over consciousness, death and consequently their rebirth. It was what meditation was finally about. We sat up. What the lamas were about to tell us were the great secrets of Tibet.

Imagine this: a great meditator is approaching death. Rather than passively lying down, waiting for the range of sensations and emotions to sweep over him or her, as most of us do, he or she sits calmly upright and, gathering the full power of supreme concentration, actually controls the consciousness as it leaves the body through the varying stages of death. Continuing that full awareness, the meditator then enters the final stage, the supremely blissful Clear Light, which marks the emergence of the most subtle mind of all. This is his or her golden chance. For in this shimmering, luminous, ecstatic state the adept can penetrate the absolute nature of reality and break the chains of karma. He or she is finally free. The goal of liberation has been reached. No longer compelled to wander in endless lives without any control, the meditator has won the state of permanent peace and happiness. Nirvana, no less.

This, the lamas said, was no fantastic Himalayan myth. It actually happened over and over again, and Tibet's history was full of accounts of such feats. The greatest among these meditators then made the supreme sacrifice. Compelled by an overwhelming compassion that could not bear to see the suffering of humankind, they willingly forsook the state of Nirvana and chose to return to this earth in order to show others the way out. In Tibet they were called the tulkus or rinpoches, the Precious Ones, for not only were they the holders of priceless wisdom, but their act of taking on another human body with the limitations and sufferings that this entailed was the noblest, bravest act of all.

As I sat at the feet of the lamas, listening to these extraordinary revelations, I thought about the remarkable stroke of fate, or karma, that had brought them to us. None of us would ever have heard these things, Tibet would have kept its secrets for ever, if the Chinese had not invaded, forcing the Dalai Lama and thousands of monks and nuns to flee to the outside world, bringing their special wisdom with them. Tibet's tragic loss was our gain. Back in 1976, when I first heard the lamas' teachings, the message was spectacularly new.

We listened agog to stories that to Lama Yeshe and Lama Zopa were commonplace. We heard how Indian officials had stood by in amazement at the sight of a Tibetan 'corpse' some three weeks old with no sign of pulse or breath, yet still sitting upright with sweet odours emanating from its body even in the heat of high summer. We heard how, back in Tibet, in the midst of destroying the sacred monasteries and artefacts the rampaging Red Guard were stopped in their tracks: prising open sacred sarcophagi, they found the bodies of long-deceased masters still intact, with their hair and nails still growing. Similarly, in the jails where so many of the monks and nuns were imprisoned and brutally tortured (a crime still being perpetuated to this day), they witnessed the remarkable sight of lamas quietly retiring to a corner of their cell, taking up the meditation position, and, without further ado, simply leaving their body. They were neither sick nor 'dying', but were practising powa, the 'transference of consciousness' technique whereby they ejected their consciousness to a different existence. Apparently hundreds of meditators performed powa at this grim time. Out in the countryside other adepts went even further – they 'died', taking their bodies with them. They had achieved what is called the Rainbow Body.

There was more. We learned of that other remarkable Tibetan 'speciality', the finding of reincarnated masters and their reinstallation in their former positions so that they could teach anew. The stories of their rebirth were every bit as fascinating as the way they had died. We heard how at the time of their death and cremation they left signs such as miniature footprints in the ashes, pointing in a certain direction, or letters and symbols appearing in the clouds of their funeral pyres, indicating where the search parties should start looking for their next life here on earth. We learned of the extensive tests given to the contenders, whereby a small reincarnated child was asked to identify his former possessions concealed among other similar and even identical objects. And we were told of the strange, precocious wisdom, the spiritual maturity of the young tulkus when their identity was verified and they resumed the mantle left off in their previous life.

I listened to all of this, and when the course was over I headed back to my London life of journalism and fast social whirl. But the words that the lamas had told me, and those hours of sitting in meditation on that remote hillside, never left me. Over the years I took time out now and again to hear their message and learn a little more of their ancient truths. I pondered on the meaning of Buddhism in general and reincarnation in particular. I was, as Lama Yeshe had exhorted, 'checking up'. Gradually I came to the conclusion that logically, at least, it made sense.

Then came the turning point. Just before dawn on the day of the Tibetan New Year, 3 March 1984, Lama Thubten Yeshe passed away. He was just forty-nine years old and I, along with thousands of Westerners whose lives he had touched, mourned. With his death reincarnation moved out of the realm of speculation and into a living reality.

One October morning in 1987, I was confronted with a small Spanish child and told quite specifically that he was the reincarnation of Lama Thubten Yeshe. Lama Zopa Rinpoche and His Holiness the Dalai Lama had both verified the fact. My mind boggled. Accepting reincarnation on an intellectual level was one thing, but accepting it in the flesh was another! To all of us who had known and loved Lama Yeshe, seeing Lama Osel as a continuation of our Tibetan teacher demanded a quantum leap. But not only were we being presented with a demonstrable proof of reincarnation, we were also being given a rinpoche, a Precious One. Could it possibly be true?

Both my professional instincts and personal curiosity were stirred by the challenge. The result was a book, *Reincarnation – the Boy Lama*. When it was published at the end of 1988 I thought that Lama Osel was the only Western rinpoche. Then, over the next few years, I heard of one or two others. They were dotted here and there across the world. Their profiles may have been decidedly lower than Lama Osel's but they were definitely out there, each with a job to do, a mission of some sort to fulfil.

My journalist's antennae began to buzz. What were they doing here? Why had they come to the West now? It was, after all, the first time in recorded history that Tibetan tulkus had been born as Westerners and recognized. Here was a reincarnation story worth telling.

As I looked, I began to suspect that what was happening very quietly was a great cosmic experiment. The new Western tulkus could only be coming for one reason – to put into our language the deepest mysteries that they had once practised in Tibet. Hadn't the Buddha said that he would manifest in whatever form was needed to benefit sentient beings? And hadn't Buddhism itself spread organically to different countries, shaping itself to the land in which it found itself? Now seemed to be the West's turn. In fact over the past few years I had noticed that Buddhism, especially Tibetan Buddhism with its deep mysteries and its laughing lamas, had been steadily increasing in popularity in the West.

It was a bold, exciting plan, but one fraught with difficulties. The rich vein of truth that lay within Tibetan Buddhism was buried within layers of culture radically different from our own. Extracting the essence from the structure that supported it would be a gargantuan, infinitely painstaking task. And if that was accomplished, could it then be successfully transplanted into our own rigorous but still rough Western souls?

As I watched and wondered I saw another trend emerging, parallel to the movement of the Eastern yogis to the West. Apart from the general interest in reincarnation some serious research into the phenomenon was being conducted. Bona fide professionals such as psychologists, university professors, counsellors and representatives of Western faiths were now investigating the possibility that we might have lived more than one life. Institutions were being set up, for example in the Netherlands and the USA, to examine the subject of reincarnation.

And overhanging this whole new movement was the great debate currently raging in science about the mind, or consciousness. Was it the same as the brain, or something else? Where did our consciousness originate? Did it come from our conception, our birth, the Big Bang or somewhere else? My antennae buzzed again. The scientists were now asking the same questions as the Buddhists.

The confluence of these two movements, one from the East, the other from the West, at the same point in time was nothing short of phenomenal. It could not be ignored. Would this recent wave of Western research validate or contradict what the lamas had taught? Would it add a new perspective, a new dimension, to the ancient teachings of the East? Could the Eastern experience and the Western view co-exist? Or would the old way of the East have to change to meet the new findings of the West?

There were so many questions that needed answering. So I decided to go on a personal exploration of reincarnation to find the new Western tulkus, to see for myself who they were and what they were doing, and to unearth for myself the recent discoveries from the West. It seemed a worthy mission.

2

TENZIN SHERAB

My travels to find the new Western tulkus brought me first of all to Tenzin Sherab, a twenty-one-year-old Canadian living in Montreal. Actually I had heard of a young Canadian rinpoche who had been at Lama Yeshe's funeral in Boulder Creek, California, some nine years earlier, but no news had reached me about him since. Certainly his voice seemed pleasant enough when I rang telling him of my quest and asking if I could meet him – but still, I wasn't sure what I would find in a young man who had been officially recognized as the reincarnation of Geshe Jatse, an eminent Tibetan sage and meditator, who had died in his cave in Tibet over thirty years ago.

It has to be said that on first appearance Tenzin Sherab bore little resemblance to an oriental yogi. The tall, slim figure who came to meet me at my hotel had the clean-cut good looks of a typical North American guy. He was dressed not in the maroon and gold robes that I had come to associate with the rinpoches, but in a pair of shorts and a T-shirt. And in place of the shining bald pate there was a full head of fine, light brown hair. Looking at him, I noticed that his face was pleasant and open, with a strong chin and wide mouth; but what caught my attention were his eyes. They were so deep-set as to be virtually hidden under a prominent, jutting brow. Trying to peer into their fathomless depths it seemed as if they told of years, if not lifetimes, of intense looking inwards. He also had an unusual protrusion in the middle of that prominent brow, which at first sight made me think he had walked into a door. Later, I fancifully wondered if it were the legacy of constantly bumping his head on the ground in the Tibetan ritual practice of full body prostrations.

On the journey back to his flat which he shares with his father, Isaac, it quickly became evident that Tenzin Sherab was not another 'regular North American guy' at all. He had a 'presence' – a quiet but assured authority and dignity that emanated from him. He also possessed that attractive mix of refinement, sensitivity and lightness of being that I had observed in other Tibetan rinpoches. It was a subtle but powerful blend. Like Lama Osel, the young Spanish boy who had been recognized as the reincarnation of Lama Yeshe, he was also exceptionally aware of others, quick to detect their feelings, anxious to accommodate their needs whenever he could.

Ensconced in his living room, I decided to ask him outright the most leading question of all – who he thought he was. It was bold but irresistible. This, after all, was the first adult rinpoche I had met, and at twenty-one he was old enough to assess for himself the validity of the reincarnation theory from first-hand experience.

'Do you feel you are the reincarnation of Geshe Jatse?' I asked.

'I *know* I am.' The reply was immediate and emphatic.

'You *know* you are?' I asked, taken aback at the spontaneity of his reply.

'Oh, yeah,' he repeated.

He went to fetch a photograph of Geshe Jatse to show me himself in his past life.

'That's me. You can't see my eyes – I was not very photo-genic,' he said, showing me a faded picture of a thin Tibetan in monk's clothing, with a long face and eyes disappearing into his head – uncannily similar to Tenzin Sherab's. I was fascinated by his automatic use of the pronouns 'me' and 'my', as though he was completely identifying with the person in the photograph. I asked him if he realized what he was saying.

'Often I spontaneously refer to him as "me". It's like he is me, you know. But I sometimes refer to Geshe Jatse as "him".

It depends. Often it's easier for someone to relate to "him" than "me". Actually, this photo has a habit of disappearing, then reappearing when you least expect it,' he added in a matter-of-fact way.

What makes him so sure than he and this man are the same, I pressed.

'There are many things that are the same about us – particularly the way we look from the nose up. The way I think, the way I feel and perceive things on an emotional and physical basis. That, I think, has stayed pretty much the same – although it might have been enhanced or changed a bit,' he replied. His confidence, his total assuredness, was much more than I had ever expected to find.

I tried to find out a little about Geshe Jatse, to get some clue as to why he had transformed himself into this tall Canadian sitting before me.

Tenzin did not know a great deal about his 'predecessor' apart from the fact that Geshe Jatse had been born in Tibet at the beginning of the twentieth century and, like so many men of that country, decided to become a monk. He rose to become the Gegu – the vice-abbot and disciplinarian – of Sera monastery in Lhasa, and was respected as a great meditator and scholar. 'He was a quietly intense, private individual, who preferred meditation to monastic politics and gossip. He had a reputation of being a character, capable of odd outbursts of idiosyncratic behaviour,' he said.

Apparently he was also a man of exceptional spiritual powers. 'I had a statue that grew teeth and another that gave nectar. They became a source of disruption, so I gave them to the monastery,' Tenzin told me rather nonchalantly.

Geshe Jatse left Sera prematurely to meditate in a cave and it is thought that he died there after the Chinese invasion. Nothing was heard of him again until Tenzin Sherab was discovered in Canada.

But why had Geshe Jatse chosen to be reborn in the West, so far from his own land and culture? No one will ever be able to know the answer with absolute certainty. One thing is sure, however. From the time he had entered the monastery Geshe Jatse would have trained himself thoroughly in the Mahayanan Buddhist principle – that one forsakes Nirvana (or, in the Western idiom, a permanent place in 'heaven') in order to return over and over again to help show all sentient beings the same way of freedom. Why he chose a land he had never seen, let alone been to, is open to discussion.

I asked Tenzin Sherab what he thought.

'Before Geshe Jatse died he said he would be reborn in a place where you would need a "sky boat" to get to. It's obviously the Western Hemisphere,' he said.

'And I can tell you one thing. This guy was completely unpredictable – almost. You didn't know what he was going to do or when he was going to do it. He just did it, and quietly. I feel that more than I've heard it. And there's a very famous prophecy in Tibet that goes "When boats fly and iron horses run on wheels then the Buddha dharma will be spread around the world." It was obvious that Geshe Jatse knew it.

'Also I probably felt the same way as I do now about wanting to help people as much as possible,' he said, lapsing into talking about Geshe Jatse as himself again. 'In order to help a society you have to be part of that society. This life I have to be a Westerner with that Tibetan knowledge,' he said.

It was pretty conclusive by now that Tenzin Sherab had no doubts whatsoever about his identity, or what he was doing on earth this time around.

The Canadians jokingly refer to their own country as 'the land of the bland', but nothing could be less banal than the remarkable story of Tenzin Sherab's 'discovery'. He was born Elijah Ary on 17 June 1972, on Sakadawa, the most auspicious date in the Tibetan calendar. This is the day which celebrates the Buddha's birth, death and Enlightenment all in one. Because Elijah was a large baby he emerged into this world by caesarian section, and although the surgeon told his parents that all was well they were alarmed by the news that their son would have to have an operation on his feet to enable him to learn to walk. For months in the womb he had had his legs crossed with the soles of his feet turned upwards, in full lotus position.

Carol and Isaac Ary had met and married young and already had a daughter by the time their son was born. Carol was a qualified nurse and Isaac owned a paint business. Like Paco and Maria, Lama Osel's parents, they had recently 'found' Tibetan Buddhism and had set up a small centre in Vancouver, where they lived. She had been brought up a Protestant, he as a 'questioning' Jew, but both were spiritual seekers who had been drawn to the esoteric teachings of the Buddha and the lamas which had just emerged from Tibet. It was an ideal choice for a Tibetan mediator wanting to be reborn in the West.

Carol, a small, lively woman now divorced from Ary, picks up the story:

'The day he was born our resident lama wanted to call him Tashi Lumpo, which is a funny name because it's the name of a monastery in Tibet. He also told us that our child was special, that he had been a monk in his previous life, that we had to take great care of him, and that we would see later. At the time, it didn't mean much to me. We just though he was being sweet and giving him a nice name. Now, looking back on it, it's clear that this was the first time Tenzin was recognized,' she said.

According to his parents, Elijah was an exceptionally serene child. 'Really angelic,' is how his mother describes him. 'As a baby he was incredible. From the day he was brought home he was exceptionally peaceful – he slept through the night. There were no problems. He was extremely easy to care for and was always very happy,' she recollected.

'There were things about him that were different. He was always observant and quiet. At the same time he was outgoing and very much involved with people. I noticed he often championed the losers, the ones who had been pushed out. He'd gravitate to them and take them in.

'He was also a pacifist, right from the start, which worked against him at school because the kids would pick on him. He'd never get involved in fights. Instead, he always tried to patch things up. Later, after he was officially recognized, the kids found out he was learning Tibetan at home and they picked on him and ostracized him. It broke my heart,' she said.

Life went on as usual in the Ary household. A second daughter was born. They moved from Vancouver to Quebec and set up another Tibetan Buddhist centre on the advice of their teacher, the late Kalu Rinpoche, a lama from the Kagyu sect, one of the four schools of Tibetan Buddhism. Kalu Rinpoche had come to the West after the fall of Tibet and set up his base in France. With his gentle wisdom and exquisite bearing, he had attracted a large following.

When they reached Montreal Isaac and Carol were told that they should contact a lama named Geshe Tenrub. The advice was to prove significant. Geshe Tenrub was from the Gelugpa sect, the school to which Geshe Jatse belonged. He would prove an important player in the search that was to follow.

During the early years many visiting lamas came to Montreal and were invited to give talks at the Arys' centre. One day when Elijah Tenzin was three years old, Tenzin Pema Jeltsen, the abbot of the newly established Drepung monastery in India, came to teach. It was to be a turning point in Elijah's life, explained Carol.

'We had many meetings in our house but we never forced the kids to go in and get involved. If they felt comfortable to come in and if they were quiet they could stay. This particular night Tenzin would keep coming in and he'd sit very quietly just staring at this guy. He was very involved with him. Towards the end of the talk I took him out and put him to bed because he was getting tired.

'As I was tucking him in I told him what a special occasion it was because Geshe Tenrub had been Tenzin Pema Jeltsen's student in Tibet, and how wonderful it was that they were together again. Suddenly Tenzin just "gave".

'He said, "I have a Geshe too." I said "Oh?", and he said, "Yes, his name is Geshe Kunawa and he lives way high up in the mountains. And he has a good friend and his name is Mahakala Nabul." Well, this was all very strange to me. He went on, "And Mahakala Nabul has a brother whose name is Om Ah Hung, and Mahakala Nabul has a knife with a skull on the end of it and he pushed it into his stomach and many, many lights came flying out, sparkling out of his stomach." Then he talked about a horse with wings and many more people with Tibetan names. He'd never done this before. It seemed it was all triggered off by Tenzin Pema Jeltsen. It was really strange. Kids always talk and they imagine, but this was very different,' she said.

'The morning after the visit I told Isaac what had occured. "Something happened last night. It was as though Tenzin was looking into another world. It was like he was dreaming, but he was awake – as though he was seeing a vision," I said.

'So we called Geshe Tenrub and Tenzin Pema Jeltsen and told them the story. Tenzin Pema Jeltsen got very excited and said, "I want to see him *now!*" So we took him over and Tenzin Pema Jeltsen looked at him and kept knocking heads with him as the Tibetans do in greeting, and presented him with a long white ceremonial scarf, the traditional sign of respect. Tenzin Pema Jeltsen then told us he not only knew *who* Tenzin was talking about but *what* he was talking about. He also said that he was going to research the matter further when he returned to India and that he would be in touch. Once again we were told Tenzin was a special child and that we should take great care of him. We said "OK" but because we could do no more at this stage we gradually let the whole thing drop.'

While the Arys might have been somewhat relaxed about what was happening, Tenzin Pema Jeltsen had a good reason to be excited. What young Elijah, or Tenzin Sherab, was demonstrating was extremely rare even among Tibetan

Buddhists. He was, in fact, recognizing himself. Without prompting, without being surrounded by the regalia and attention that come after official recognition, Tenzin Sherab was automatically giving names, places, details and events of a former existence completely of his own accord. To the cognoscenti, this ability placed Tenzin high on the spiritual evolution ladder.

If this whole episode was pushed to the back of Carol's and Isaac's minds it had ignited something which continued to burn with ever-increasing intensity within their son. From the moment of meeting Tenzin Pema Jeltsen, every night for the next four years he travelled in his mind to a place he called his 'planet'. There he saw strange and curious things: vast mountains – much higher than those which surrounded him in Canada; dusty roads, peculiar houses, animals, different types of trees. He had teachers and friends there whose names he knew, and he also had a protector, a strange and beautiful horse with wings. He described it all, in vivid and specific detail, over and over again to his family.

He was so convinced that his planet was real and that he truly went there that one night he persuaded his curious but fearful sisters to travel there with him. The preparations were all made. Sandwich boxes were filled, warm clothes put on (for Elijah said it was cold there), and the three of them settled down in Elijah's bed ready for the journey. The next morning the girls looked at each other and declared in disdain there was no such place as Elijah's 'planet'. Elijah was crestfallen. 'Didn't you see it? Because I did,' he said.

Today, at twenty-one, Elijah/Tenzin is still positive that what he was doing was 'remembering'. 'I don't like saying they were dreams, because to me they were reality. It's true they came in dream form, but in my mind there is no doubt that they were real – I was recollecting. Later, when I was shown a picture of Tibet, I recognized my "planet" immediately,' he said.

In the meantime, Tenzin Pema Jeltsen had been conducting some research into the identity of the disciple of Geshe

Kunawa; but before he made his announcement the Dalai
Lama came to Montreal. Elijah had an audience with him. As
he walked into the room the Dalai Lama looked up, pointed
a finger at the seven-year-old in front of him and burst out,
much to the astonishment of all present, 'I know who you
are! You are the reincarnation of Geshe Jatse!'

By an extraordinary coincidence someone pressed a camera
shutter at that precise moment, recording for posterity the
spontaneous gesture of recognition by the Dalai Lama. It is
there in Tenzin Sherab's possession – as concrete an item of
proof as you can get in this ultimately non-material field of
reincarnation. It shows the Dalai Lama standing· in front of
a statue of Buddha in a shrine room in Montreal. Before him
is the young Elijah Ary, in jeans and sweater, being ushered
forward by a Tibetan monk; the Dalai Lama is pointing his
finger straight at the boy with an expression of surprised
delight.

Shortly afterwards, the Dalai Lama gave Elijah Ary the
name of Tenzin Sherab. It was at that moment that his dual life
as a Tibetan reincarnation in a Western land really began.

At the time suddenly being called a 'reincarnation' of a
Tibetan spiritual adept did not have much meaning for the
eight-year-old Tenzin. In fact he had no idea what the Dalai
Lama was talking about.

'I thought he was talking about a flower – something to
do with a carnation,' he recalled with a laugh. 'I kept trying
to figure out what everyone was talking about. At one level
I guess I knew – because I had this awareness that I was
somehow different. But on another level I wasn't aware of
the issue of reincarnation as such.'

Nevertheless, as he grew up Tenzin Sherab continued to
demonstrate that he was indeed different – that he possessed
a special knowledge that other children did not have. This
kept showing itself in a variety of ways.

There was the occasion when Isaac decided to explain to
Tenzin the meaning of the seven offering bowls that were

put on the altar in front of the Buddha. This, Isaac explained to me, was not because he wanted to instil in Tenzin the minutiae of Buddhist ritual. Quite the contrary. He was intent on clarifying what each bowl represented precisely because he did not want his son to get caught up in mindless worship.

Summoning his young son to him, he very carefully went through the specific offerings or gifts that each bowl stood for. 'This represents water for washing the feet. This water for drinking. This flowers. This perfume. This music. This food. And this last bowl represents light,' he said, looking at Tenzin to see if he comprehended.

'That's right,' Tenzin confirmed, and walked out.

And there was the time when the family were out walking in the woods, and his father was swinging him by the arms. Suddenly he looked at his father and announced, 'I used to do this to you when I was your father and you were a small child.'

Isaac was astounded. 'When you were my father, where did we live?' he asked.

'In the mountains,' Tenzin replied, and described the place to him. Not surprisingly, it was Tibet.

This revelation was especially fascinating because it seemed to prove what the Tibetan lamas had often told us, that we were frequently reborn to people whom we had known in the past – those with whom we had karmic connections.

Perhaps nowhere did Tenzin demonstrate his affinity with his past life more than he did with the lamas who continued to visit Carol and Isaac's centre. He wanted to be with them all the time and cried inconsolably for days after they had left. According to his parents, he would be so upset that it would take them two weeks to calm him down.

It was not entirely surprising, therefore, that even before he was officially recognized Tenzin Sherab voiced a desire to become a monk. He was eight when he met the Karmapa, head of the Kagyu sect and an extremely famous rinpoche in his own right.

'I said to the Karmapa, "I want to be a monk just like you."

'He replied, "But you will miss your parents."

'And I said, "Yeah, but it's all right." It's important to know what's in store. I knew, and it didn't bother me.'

Meanwhile back in Sera monastery, in India, the lamas had independently carried out their own investigations, including consulting the State Oracle, a monk who, in trance, delivers messages from those forces from beyond which are committed to the protection of Tibet. Once they were convinced that Tenzin was indeed Geshe Jatse reborn, they sent robes to him in Canada along with urgent requests for him to be sent to them. But at this stage the Arys were not prepared to give up their young son to a Tibetan monastery in India which they had never seen, and Tenzin himself was not ready to go. They consulted the Dalai Lama and Kalu Rinpoche, both of whom reassured them that the time was not yet right.

Nevertheless, Tenzin Sherab was on track – albeit in his Western culture. He took his preliminary vows in Canada at the age of nine and took refuge with His Holiness the Dalai Lama in 1980. This meant acceptance into the monastic system. When the occasion demanded it, he wore with pride the robes that the Sera monks had sent him, but he did not shave his head (although he did so when he went to France to visit Kalu Rinpoche).

Around this time there was another important milestone in Tenzin Sherab's unusual life, as Carol recalled.

'The Dalai Lama was giving the Kalachakra Initiation in Montreal, and we weren't going to go. Then I got this incredible urge that we should attend – it was as if a hand was pushing my back. So we went, and Tenzin was so happy. At the Kalachakra we met a monk who had been a student of Geshe Jatse – he really wanted to meet Tenzin, and had all sorts of questions he wanted to ask.

'Well, Tenzin became really stern with this man – who was now a geshe in his own right. He became like an old man. He sat in a chair with his legs crossed, just staring at this man, staring really intensely. I'd never seen him look at anyone like that before. At that moment he wasn't a nine-year-old at all. He didn't offer respect, or make himself "lower" as the custom should be for a child who was meeting someone older. It was as if Tenzin was in the superior position.

'This monk told us that the Geshe Kunawa whom Tenzin had talked about on his "planet" had indeed been Geshe Jatse's teacher in Tibet. He also told us about the "horse with wings" that Tenzin saw regularly on his "planet". Apparently Geshe Jatse had a protector called Hayagriva – who is a horse-headed winged tantric deity. Geshe Jatse had done many retreats and meditational practices on Hayagriva. And we thought he had been talking about Pegasus! Suddenly many of the things that Tenzin repeatedly talked about began to make sense.'

In his many meetings with remarkable men that marked his early life Tenzin also happened to encounter Lama Yeshe – the man who, unknown to anyone at that time, was himself preparing for a Western rebirth. Could it have been coincidence, I wondered: After all, both Tenzin Sherab and Lama Osel were spearheads in this extraordinary movement in the world's spiritual history – the transplanting of the ancient truths of Buddhism from the East to the West. Both Lama Yeshe and Geshe Jatse had been to Sera monastery in Tibet.

Certainly Lama Yeshe immediately recognized Tenzin Sherab, much the same as the Dalai Lama did. The meeting took place during a visit by Tenzin to Vajrapani, Lama Yeshe's centre in the middle of the redwood forests at Boulder Creek in California. Tenzin Sherab, then a small boy, was ushered into the room where Lama Yeshe was delivering the Buddha dharma in his own incomparable style, and sat quietly among all the others. Without interrupting the flow of his speech or looking at Tenzin Sherab Lama Yeshe suddenly said, 'We have a young tulku in our midst', and pointed at the young boy in blue jeans and short-sleeved blue shirt. Lama Yeshe's clairvoyant skills must have been at work here, since Tenzin Sherab had not yet been officially recognized.

Although Tenzin Sherab only saw Lama Yeshe once, the connection between them was strong. 'We got on amazingly well. The first thing I noticed about him was the big gap in his front teeth. He told me about Geshe Jatse, whom he hadn't met but certainly knew of. He said he was an amazing teacher and a skilled meditator. He said that Geshe Jatse would sit in meditation for days, not touching the food that people brought to him.

'The last time I saw Lama Yeshe I and my sister and a friend were playing with some bulrushes when he appeared and started talking to me about my future. Unfortunately I don't remember the exact words he used – but he gave me advice about later on in life. I'm pretty sure I'm not remembering it now because I shouldn't. It's not time yet. I do remember he said, "Study well." Those were the last words he spoke to me.

'A few months later we received a telephone call from Vajrapani. My mother picked up the phone, and I looked at her and said, "Lama Yeshe has died, hasn't he?"

'She said, "How did you know?"

'"I felt it." I said. Even though I hardly knew him, I felt so close to him.'

A week after Lama Yeshe had passed away Tenzin Sherab made the long journey back to California to attend Lama Yeshe's cremation on the hill at Vajrapani. There he was to reveal his special powers again. According to the Tibetan Buddhist tradition, when a high lama is cremated he will leave signs which not only indicate the validity of his spiritual accomplishments but also give directions and clues about his next incarnation. The students at Vajrapani had dutifully built their first stupa, an ornate edifice whose dimensions represented the enlightened mind, into which they had reverently placed the upright body of Lama Yeshe before setting it alight. When the flames had subsided, the stupa was opened for the relics to be examined and signs to be found. Tenzin takes up the story.

'I remember at that moment I was playing with my watch and I saw a reflection of the clouds in it. I decided to look up, just like that, and I saw all these Tibetan images and letters going by. There was a Sa and a Ma and I told that to Lama Zopa. He thanked me for the information and it turned out that Sa was for Spain, the country where Lama Osel was to be born, and Ma was his intended mother's name – Maria.'

Later, when he was in Sera monastery, his path crossed again with Lama Yeshe, albeit in his new form as Lama Osel. In spite of the age gap, the affinity was instantaneous. 'He's definitely the continuation of Lama Yeshe. We get along so well. He used to pull me into his room to play with him and read his comics with him. It's as though now he treats me as an older brother,' he said.

While he was at Vajrapani verification he met His Holiness Tsong Rinpoche, who had been called in to conduct the funeral proceedings. After it was over he invited Tenzin and Isaac Ary to join him in his room. This was an honour but also somewhat intimidating, as Tsong Rinpoche was not only an eminent high lama but a rather grand figure not given to outward displays of bonhomie like Lama Yeshe. On the way back to Tsong Rinpoche's room his translator disappeared, leaving Tenzin and Isaac alone with the master and without any means of communication.

They sat there in silence for what seemed a long time when, much to Isaac's horror, Tenzin suddenly stood up and, without saying anything, prostrated himself to Tsong Rinpoche before walking out. It was a big breach of manners and protocol. Tsong Rinpoche, however, didn't bat an eyelid. Isaac tells what happened next.

'The attendant came back and Tsong Rinpoche immediately began to speak in Tibetan. The attendant translated: "Rinpoche says that in your son's previous life he was Rinpoche's cousin." This was a fact I didn't know. "Rinpoche says that the last time he saw him he was sitting in his house and your son came in and sat down, and didn't say anything for about half an hour. Then he got up, prostrated himself and walked out. Rinpoche says your son has not changed much!"'

As Isaac recalled the incident Tenzin cried with laughter at the memory. 'Some things never change,' he repeated, tears rolling down his face.

In amongst the laughter and warmth of his early family life there were also moments of sadness. Somehow Tenzin knew he had a destiny, one that would cost him dearly.

'When he was about nine I found him crying,' recalled Carol. 'He showed me a letter he'd written to a lama at Sera. It read, "Dear Karma Thinley, I can't resist my karma. I love you, Tenzin."

'I said to him, "What's all this about? Why are you crying?"

'He replied, "I'm crying because I can't resist my karma."

'I asked him again what he meant, and he said, "One day I'm going to have to leave you and the family and go back to the monastery."'

At this point Carol told him emphatically he didn't have to do anything he didn't want to do, nor go anywhere he didn't want to go.

'"No," he said quietly, "I'll go. I'll have to go one day."' And he was right.

To be born as a reincarnation of a Tibetan spiritual master in a Western land is a curious destiny. But it is one that Geshe Jatse and presumably his new-found persona as Elijah Ary aka Tenzin Sherab chose freely and willingly in order to fulfil certain purposes in the scheme of things.

As he foresaw when he was a boy, the day came when Tenzin Sherab did return to his monastery, now established in southern India. For some years the Arys had been resisting the pleas from Sera 'to send us our lama', but when he was fourteen word came from the Dalai Lama that it was time for Tenzin to go. Kalu Rinpoche independently gave the same advice. So, trusting in the word of these wise and great beings, and having assured themselves that Tenzin was willing, the Arys finally allowed their son to be immersed totally in the Tibetan monastic framework. One day in 1986 Tenzin set off to another world and another vital chapter in his extraordinary life.

Sera, with its 2500 monks living in what is virtually a small town in a patch of cleared out jungle in southern India, is the biggest monastery in the world. There Tenzin was, in his own words, 'a grain of sand upon a beach'. By the time he left Sera that sea of Tibetan culture included just ten Westerners, one of whom was Lama Osel Rinpoche.

It was a huge step for all concerned – one that reflected the dilemma and difficulties involved in this new phenomenon of Eastern tulkus coming to the West.

'We come from a Western tradition and, even though we were followers of Tibetan Buddhism, we were critical to some degree. We knew that the monastery benefited financially when a tulku entered – so that thought crossed my mind. Also, I was worried about the hygiene and the harsh conditions of India,' said Carol.

Isaac, always a questioning man, had his own misgivings. 'It's quite difficult to send your son to a monastery that you've never been to and where you don't know anyone. And I have always been wary about mindless ritual. In every religion there are snags people get into – I don't want to step on anyone's toes, but I've seen Westerners who tend to grovel and worship when they get into Eastern religions. I didn't want Tenzin too caught up in that.'

They need not have worried. Tenzin fitted into Tibetan monastic life as if he had been born to it! He was instantly at home. It was taken as yet another indication that he was indeed the reincarnation of Geshe Jatse – the former Gegu of Sera.

Tenzin mastered Tibetan, an extremely difficult language, within weeks and in just three months was fluent enough to be debating complex points of Buddhist philosophy with other monks. Within a year he had no accent whatsoever and it was said that, if he had his back to you, there was no way of telling he was not Tibetan.

He also memorized Tibetan prayers and scriptures at the same remarkable speed. 'The lamas said it was because I'd studied them in a past life,' said Tenzin modestly. 'There were a few that I just remembered off hand. I heard them once or twice and I could recite them along with everyone else.'

From the moment he walked into Sera, proof of his identity came spontaneously from several sources. The older monks, who had known Geshe Jatse, were immediately taken aback by the physical resemblance between Tenzin Sherab and their former master. 'They said that I looked just the same from the middle of my nose up,' commented Tenzin, referring to that highly distinctive jutting out forehead and his exceptionally deep-set eyes.

'The Tibetans actually saw me as a Tibetan and not as a Westerner. That was nice. It made me feel accepted,' he continued. Their acceptance of him was not surprising since scholastically he was passing out top of his class, the Buddhist hierarchy's acid test of the authenticity of an incarnation.

To allay their fears, his family made a trip to India to see him. Said Carol: 'It wasn't until I went to the monastery that I saw for myself that they weren't after Tenzin for any financial gain they thought he might bring. Tenzin had fitted in brilliantly. It was like putting a fish into water. The conditions there were, as I'd imagined, pretty tough, but he never got really ill or had any major problems. He loved the way of life – particularly the debate. When I first took him there, before he could speak Tibetan, he would hang over the fence watching the monks argue and discuss, absolutely enthralled,' she said.

For six years Tenzin lived out his life as a Tibetan monk steeped in the richness, power and rigidity of a spiritual system which has stayed intact for hundreds of years. Although he did well there were inevitably times when he looked back to his Canadian life with longing. But even these moments he managed to turn into part of his training.

'A couple of times I resented being so far from home – occasions when I needed my parents and they weren't around, they were miles from where I was. I had a sense of abandonment. It was like an emotional slap across the face which made me wake up and say, "That's not what you're here for."'

During the years he was steeped in this all-encompassing world he grew both spiritually and personally. He learned the profound truths of the nature of the mind and then of all existence. He learned about himself and his vast potential to expand his mind to total omniscience and total compassion – if only he could eradicate for all time the negativities or 'delusions' which sullied this pure and blissful state. He learned extraordinary self-discipline, for Tibetan monasteries impose a regimen which could make an army camp seem lax. But, if what they said about Tenzin Sherab was true – that he was the reincarnation of Geshe Jatse – then he was not really learning these things, merely remembering in order to put them into force yet again in his current lifetime.

If his previous life had been that of a Tibetan holy man who died in a cave while meditating, this time round he was indubitably a Westerner. His origins would not lie down, and there were aspects of his life at Sera with which he openly disagreed. Like his father Isaac, or maybe because of him, Tenzin could never accept the entire Tibetan monastic system without question. He was going on his own path.

'They used to call me "the rebel" at Sera because I bucked the system,' said Tenzin. 'It happened from the moment I stepped foot in the place. They held this huge ceremony to welcome me there and started to explain what I should do, and when I said, "Why are you having this ritual anyway? Why make it so complicated? I'm just me, and I'm going into the monastery.' And they didn't really have an answer.

'I used to ask those sorts of questions a lot, and the only answer I would get was, "It's tradition." It *is* tradition, and old habits died hard.' For the young monk from the New World this was hard to take. From the outset he resisted many of the cultural aspects of Tibetan Buddhism, particularly the strong emphasis on obeisance. Increasingly it began to irk him.

'I kept saying, "You have to change in order to appeal to

the times. You have to change with them." But they wouldn't accept it. It's amazing how opposed they are to change, which is kind of ironic because one of the Buddha's main teachings is that everything is impermanent,' he said.

From Canada also came influxes of his native culture, nurturing the Western side of his nature. His sisters, Leila and Bryna, sent him bundles of literature on feminism, in which they were keenly involved, while from other sources came the latest publications on computer technology. Tenzin lapped it all up. Then after he had finished a particular set of exams he made a trip back to Montreal, where the life of his homeland strengthened in him afresh the influences of his birthplace.

Inevitably the two streams that were flowing through his present incarnation – his Western roots and his destiny – converged, and one day he knew that his path lay in the West.

'I was reborn as a Westerner to bridge the two cultures. But it's not as simple as that. It's that, but it's also something more. It's to help a process of healing – emotional healing. I don't know what to call it. I want to help people understand the message of Tibetan Buddhism, which is peace, harmony, love and compassion between all people of the world.

'I felt I had to take what Tibetan Buddhism has to offer and put it into Western terms. It's like taking something and shaping it differently to put it in another place. You can take a piece of dough and make it into a circle or make it into a square – the shape changes, but it's still the same material. The essence stays the same.'

He was just eighteen when the meaning of why he had been born struck him. 'Before that moment,' he continued, 'I didn't know why I was here or why I was at Sera. Gradually I understood what I should do in order to achieve my final goal.'

From then on he knew he had to leave the cloistered world of Sera monastery. His place was in the West. This was a radical and brave step, for he was supposed to stay in India for at least another five years to finish his geshe studies, and considerable pressure was put on tulkus to live up to all expectations. But Tenzin had made up his mind – he only needed the Dalai Lama's permission. In his heart he knew he could not leave without the great man's blessing.

He set off alone on the long journey from the tip of the subcontinent to Dharamsala in the Himalayan foothills, where the Dalai Lama had established his government-in-exile, to tell the head of Tibetan Buddhism, the man venerated as a living Buddha, what he had decided to do. When he walked into the room the Dalai Lama said: 'What are you doing here? I thought you were going to university in the West!' And his visitor rather quietly said that that was precisely what he had come to speak to him about. It was all the endorsement Tenzin needed. The Dalai Lama went on to suggest that Tenzin should study Western psychology, so as to understand the Western approach to the mind and to be in a better position to help others – for ultimately, what else was there to do if you were a Mahayana Buddhist than to work tirelessly throughout all incarnations helping others? If the lamas at Sera were shocked and disappointed by Tenzin's decision, the Dalai Lama's attitude was definitely more open. From the start he had never had any preconceived ideas about how Tenzin should lead his life. He knew that the young man would, and should, make up his own mind.

Carol remembers clearly the invaluable advise the Dalai Lama gave her even before Tenzin went to Sera monastery. 'He said, "You can guide them, you can advise them, but you must never, ever try to stop them when they try to do something because they know better than we know what they have to do." He went on to say that if Tenzin had the ability to predict where he was going to be reborn in this life, and then recognize himself – which he did by telling *us* of his past life – then he certainly had the ability to know how he had to go about this life. Tenzin knew what he needed to experience in order to achieve what he had to this time round,' she said. In the decidedly difficult business of bringing up a tulku, the Dalai Lama's words were a great comfort.

It was April 1992 when Tenzin finally walked out of his Tibetan monastery and back into his Western life. But even though he had rejected his monastic existence, at no time did he ever doubt that he was the reincarnation of Geshe Jatse. 'Far from it. Nor was I turning my back on everything that had happened to me so far,' Tenzin said emphatically.

Two months after he arrived back in Montreal, he handed back his robes. He had been a Tibetan Buddhist monk for twelve years. His re-entry into North American life was to prove as strange and challenging to him as his entry into Sera. But it did not deter him one bit.

If Tenzin knew in his own mind that his destiny lay in the West, forging the right path to achieve his goal was not so simple. His first necessity in the harsh world of Western commerce was to get a job. This was a difficult business for a Western tulku who, for the past six years, had been bowed to, revered and regarded as something of a spiritual prince, and trained to adopt a position of authority and power. When he had phoned Carol and Isaac from Dharamsala after his audience with the Dalai Lama, telling them he was coming home, their response was that there was always a place for him with them but that whatever decision he made he had to be accountable for it. He was not going to return to live off other people and do nothing with his life!

With the recession and unemployment, and Tenzin's complete lack of Western qualifications, doors did not open to him as readily as they had done in Sera. He may have had the highest spiritual qualifications, but from an earthly point of view his CV was unimpressive. What good was a thorough understanding of Buddhism in the professional and commercial market of Montreal? So for seven months he walked the streets looking for a job, any job, that would give him some money to live.

'It's tough to look for a job for months on end. No kidding! On top of that I didn't have any unemployment insurance. There are a lot of pressures here – having to do things you don't feel like doing, such as work,' Tenzin conceded with a laugh. 'I can see now that there is such a struggle for money here, but it's a necessity, so you can't do anything about it.' He was about to give up when his sister got a job working in a small shop selling tobacco and magazines, and asked her boss if he would employ her brother too. 'She asked maybe ten times. Finally he agreed to meet me and he hired me, because he was interested in Buddhism and psychology. With me things often happen at the last minute,' Tenzin said philosophically.

He now knows what it is like to be physically tired from standing on his feet all day, to catch people stealing, to throw them out when they become a nuisance. The shop is in a rough area of Montreal and he now regularly encounters kids on drugs and those who are mentally disturbed. It could have been a big come-down for someone used to an elite position in a Tibetan monastery, but Tenzin is taking it all in his stride. 'Oh, it's not so bad,' he comments philosophically.

But if Tenzin has suddenly been caught up in the mundane world of earning a living, his sense of destiny is as strong as ever. With the Dalai Lama's last words to him still echoing in his mind, and his own vision that he must somehow help people in his own culture, he has enrolled in the Religious Science Department of Quebec University to gain a thorough grounding in Western spiritual thought. Part of the course involves studying Freud, Jung and the other founders of modern psychology – and so another edict from the Dalai Lama is being fulfilled. He has also been invited to appear in a film about his life – a movie which he hopes will hold messages for the public about spiritual truths.

The precise format of that destiny might still be in embryonic form, but his overall vision of being of service in the world is clear. He is concerned about peace and about the pain and suffering of the world, and wants to be of assistance.

'Really, what I'd like to do is help people in any way possible, whoever they may be, whatever they may do, wherever they may be. I'm not sure in which way. I'd say more emotionally than just mentally or physically.' The words were spoken with infinite sincerity.

'If I can help someone understand themselves and hence understand others, I'm helping that person and others in a large way. It's where most of the religions are linked, the "Love thy neighbour as thyself" theme. I like to call it "global warming" because it's a warming of the heart towards others,' he said.

There are some aspects of his monastic schooling which he thinks might come in useful. 'Although all the major religions have this same message, I feel Tibetan Buddhism has something different to offer in that it allows people to question and speculate and so make up their own minds by coming to their own conclusions. I hope to be a bit of an eye-opener in that respect,' he said.

How does he feel about being a layman after all those years of being a monk? Giving back his robes might have been an essential part of being reintegrated into the West, but it could not have been done lightly. After all, he had worn those maroon and gold robes for twelve years and they had become not only his emblem of vocation but also a form of protection.

'I thought it would be easy, but it was far from easy. It took me a long time to decide exactly when I should give them back and how,' he admitted.

Gone, too, is the ritual which he found so tedious in Sera, and the sitting in meditation, the reading of the scriptures and the other business of formal religious life which occupied him for so long. The outward display of spiritual practice, he says, no longer concerns him.

'I rarely meditate now. I don't feel I need to. If I do, then I'll meditate. I'm now integrating Tibetan Buddhism into my lifestyle. The way I think, the way I act. Things I do or don't do. So I'm in practice every day, even though it doesn't seem to be.'

When pressed, he expounds further: 'I am constantly working on myself – clearing up my own muck! I like to watch my emotions. I'll watch a situation as a third person, almost, and examine it – so I'm analysing both points of view. That helps a lot. I think that is one of the tulku's gifts, being able to work with your own self and at the same time help others.

'For example, one of the most important things is learning about your own anger, and getting rid of it, because if you want peace in the world and peace between people you have to have tolerance. And tolerance is an absence of anger. Look at the trouble in Yugoslavia. Look at Monica Seles, the tennis player who got stabbed. So much trouble and suffering is caused by anger,' he explained.

'Getting rid of frustration, too, is a big step. I have found it helps to know the difference between anger and frustration so that you can identify which one you are suffering under. The Dalai Lama helped me a lot there in some teachings he gave at Mungod. With anger there's more violence. It's stronger. It feels different.

'The last time I got angry was with my sister when she said something that really upset me. It was the first time I'd got angry in so long that I couldn't even remember the time before that. I lashed out and hit a door and broke a knuckle! I took it as a reminder: "Now you know what anger is and how it can hurt. So rectify the problem,"' he admitted. 'Generally, though, I'm pretty patient,' he added.

Like the great Lama Yeshe who shook off so much of the outer trappings of Tibetan Buddhism to get to its heart, Tenzin Sherab is also in the throes of personalizing his spiritual path. His altar, like Lama Yeshe's, bears the distinct mark of individuality.

'It's the message, not the form, that matters. It's not the image that counts,' he insists. 'You should put on your altar things that are special to you, that have meaning. I have pictures of my family up there, a crystal pyramid that was given to me by Tsong Rinpoche, and a glass tube given to me on my birthday by a friend in France. I also have a three-dimensional jigsaw puzzle in the form of a diamond. My father gave it to me for Christmas, and that's special to me because it was the first Christmas I had spent with my family in so many years. I have all those little things. It's very personal.'

In the meantime, Tenzin is slipping back into the North American way of life. He's taken up that archetypal Canadian pursuit, ice hockey, revered in his country almost to the point of being a religion. He enjoys it. He laps up vampire movies and Larson cartoons, and he has a girlfriend. After teenage years marked by vows of celibacy, this is definitely foraying into unknown pastures. When most boys of his age were learning how to date and how to react romantically to the opposite sex, Tenzin was immersed in monastic discipline and the learning of Buddhism. Those who know Tenzin say he's a little unsophisticated in some social areas, the result of being closeted in a Tibetan monastery for so long, but he says he is enjoying this new-found freedom.

'It's very nice to have someone to talk to and be with other than your family,' he says. But, whether it is his age, or his earlier lifetimes as a monk, the notion of marriage and becoming a family man has no appeal whatsoever.

'It appeals to me even less than having to go through university again,' he laughs. 'I've already worked to the equivalent of having a bachelor degree, but it's not recognized here, so I have to go through the system again. That doesn't appeal to me *that* much – but to be a family man appeals to me a lot less,' he says.

It would be reasonable to think that someone who had been singled out from childhood as a special person, who had been ordained as a monk since he was nine, and who had spent years in a Tibetan monastery would find it difficult to become, on the surface at least, an ordinary Canadian citizen. Tenzin says that overall he is not having much trouble. Being adaptable, he claims, is part of what it means to be a tulku. He spoke of the art of becoming immersed in whatever it is he's doing, while still remaining apart.

'This life – this Canadian life – is a game. It's probably the same everywhere. Therefore I play hockey, I watch movies, I have a girlfriend, I work in a store, I can make a movie and still watch my mind. Once you learn how to play the game you can just play it and still go about your own business at the same time. But you have to understand the game, study it, learn it and adapt yourself to be able to function within that game. And not be noticed. You mustn't be too noticeable, too outstanding. That's what I do.'

He was a most unusual young man.

Before I left, there were a few more pressing questions I needed to put to Tenzin Sherab and his parents about reincarnation. Perhaps the most crucial concerned the extent to which Tenzin had been conditioned. After all, like any other tulku he had been taken at a very early age and moulded within the Tibetan spiritual framework. Would his gifts and abilities have emerged if he had been left entirely to his own devices?

I asked Tenzin if he felt he would have lived his life differently had he not been recognized as the reincarnation of Geshe Jatse. Now, at some distance from the monastic tradition, he was in the perfect position to judge.

'I think I would be exactly the same – with the wish to help people. A lot comes from my past life, you know,' came the instant reply. He had, he said, absolutely no regrets about being a monk or spending all those years at Sera. In fact he thought it had served him well. 'I probably would have had the same view, but it would have come a lot later and on a smaller scale. It wouldn't have been so strong. And I probably wouldn't know how to go about doing it. If I hadn't gone to Sera I would know less about myself, my emotions, my values and, of course, Buddhism than I know now. The progress would have been a lot slower. If I'd stayed in Canada I would have been caught up in the rat race, with my nose to the grindstone. I wouldn't have had time to look at how I ticked. There I learned how to do it. Also, I could have got into a lot of things like alcohol or drugs or being lazy if I'd stayed here.'

But many people, I suggested, would say he had been

brainwashed by all those years as a Tibetan monk. That his path had been set for him, that his mind had been moulded. This idea made him irate.

'I haven't been brainwashed! Far from it! If I'm conditioned it's of my own doing. If it weren't for the monastery I wouldn't be like I am now. I'm glad I went. I'm a free, independent thinker. Very much so,' he insisted.

Looking back, he conceded that being a tulku had been tough at times. 'There were times when I felt forced. Forced to learn, forced to memorize texts and prayers. That was difficult, because whenever I'm told I have to do something I'm inclined to say "No". Or else at the monastery I'd say "Yeah" but I wouldn't do it. And there are a lot of expectations put on you, especially by the Tibetans and former students, even though they may not realize it. I had to be the best student of the class, the best in this and the best in that. I had to be quiet and very calm. I just had to be the perfect person. No one's perfect. When you're not, they can get disappointed. Lama Osel has a lot of pressure on him too,' he replied.

He told me about the stress that both he and his family felt when he was young and the lamas were constantly urging for him to be sent to them. 'The year they started sending letters was the year I developed asthma, and I've had it ever since. Now that I'm out of the monastery it's getting better. I'm not saying it's a bad place, but the pressure they put on you is very heavy,' he admitted.

I asked him if he still felt he had to live up to these expectations – if they were colouring or controlling his life in any way.

Again, the response was vehement.

'No, no no! I certainly do not live up to the expectations of others. I have never done that. I live up to my own expectations', he asserted. 'In fact I hardly have any expectations of myself. I let myself go and I experience things. If I do something I do as much as I can, and if I can't do more than that I expect people to accept it.'

The answer was good enough.

There were other sticky questions about reincarnation which I wanted to have cleared up, like why he did not have precise memories of Geshe Jatse.

'The theory I have is that it's like a series of lines. Birth, death – birth, death. At birth you're closer to your previous life. At about the age of seven you begin to realize what's happening around you and you get caught up more with this life than with the last one. That happened to me, but I wasn't as conscious of it happening as I am now, looking back,' he replied.

If lives can be viewed as a series of existences, there was a time lapse of about thirty years between his incarnation as Geshe Jatse and his incarnation as Tenzin Sherab. What did he think he was doing? Where was he then?

'Some people think I might have taken another rebirth and died very young, which is possible. Some people say I was in another place, another realm. There's no real explanation. My thought is that I was reborn again and either not recognized or taken in as a monk, not officially recognized and died very young,' he said.

Then there are questions about the obvious personality differences between Geshe Jatse and Tenzin Sherab. Geshe Jatse was conservative and rather anti-social. Tenzin Sherab is clearly gregarious, happy to be the subject of a book and a film, and prepared to meet the glare of publicity head on. How does he account for such a marked contrast?

'It happens quite a lot,' he replied, nonplussed. 'There's a tulku in Sera who used to be my classmate. He was really, really thin. And in his previous life he was enormous! I saw a picture of him. I've never seen a fatter person in my life. I'm surprised he could even move around. So a lot of the time physical things and the way you act changes. Sometimes they go into opposites,' he said. Like all Tibetan-trained lamas, he always had an answer!

I turned to Carol and Isaac to see if, in retrospect, they would have handled their son's life any differently. Looking back on their decision to send Tenzin to Sera, Carol now has few regrets.

'We certainly didn't coerce him into going – he went of his own accord. It wasn't bad. I see what it's done for him. It's really made him strong. I think if he had studied in the West he would have become a lazy teenager. There he was forced to work, compete and get involved. And he loved it. It was what he needed at the time. I don't think he could do what he's doing now if he hadn't gone through that.

'Still, there was no way he was going to be a conventional lama. Before he went to Sera he said to the Dalai Lama that he didn't know if he wanted to stay a monk and be in the monastery for the rest of his life. And the Dalai Lama said it was his decision.

'Now he's free to do what he has to do. The karma he couldn't resist was, I believe, to spend some years at the monastery, because in his past life as Geshe Jatse he had left Sera prematurely to go into retreat in the mountains. He had to pay back that karma. At least, that's how I see it,' she said.

I asked her, how, having given birth to a child who supposedly has special qualities, and lived through the day-to-day life of bringing him, she now saw reincarnation.

'I see it like the story of Mozart,' she replied. 'Mozart in a way was a tulku. He grew up in an environment of music, but he also had this incredible gift and, because he was in the environment, he learned how to use that gift. I see Tenzin in the same way. A tulku is a gifted person who has the ability, given the right opportunity, to do something beneficial for themselves and others. If the opportunity is not there, they might not do it. Westerners have this mystical idea of a tulku as someone who knows everything. Well, that's not true. Tenzin makes mistakes like everybody else.

'I respect Tenzin,' she continued, 'and sometimes I see in him this really old person that I call his old spirit. Looking back at how the pieces have all fitted together, I can see that there's definitely something going on. It wasn't just a figment of my imagination or a political plot on the part of the Tibetans.'

I asked her what she thought Tenzin's particular gift was.

'Tenzin's gift is his intelligence and his ability to bring what Buddhism has to offer the modern world. But because he is a pioneer it isn't easy. He has to test the ground. Maybe the tulku system will fail, maybe it won't. Tenzin might eventually decide to go back to the monastery. It's up to him. It's his life,' she said.

Isaac saw his son more simply. 'Tenzin teaches me,' he said. 'It's like the Tibetan teachers of old who would take a pupil only when they were humbly and properly ready. The teacher would sit on one side of the tree and the pupil on the other, not seeing each other. The teacher would say nothing. The pupil would go into deep meditation, and when the master felt the student was ready he would say something that would increase his understanding and insight. That is what Tenzin does with me. I can be ruminating over a problem or an issue for days without saying anything, and then Tenzin will say something for apparently no reason. It's something I can always accept.'

And so right now Tenzin is happy with where he is and what he is doing. Life might be harder and more uncertain now that he has left the secure path that Sera monastery offered him, but he has no regrets about his decision to leave.

'I was ready to come back to the West, to reintegrate myself into a Western society. I felt that in Sera I wasn't doing much for other people,' he said.

After meeting him and hearing his story I hoped he would find his destiny in the West, whatever form it would take. And part of me secretly hoped it would be glorious. He had so much to live up to.

There was one last question to ask. Since it seemed he had the ability to choose his lives as he willed, what had he in mind for the next one?

'I'm enjoying this life – I wouldn't mind repeating it,' came the non-committal reply.

3

ROGER WOOLGER

Do we really live more than one life? Is there, in fact, a continuity of consciousness that goes from existence to existence, as the Eastern religions hold? Or is reincarnation merely an oriental belief, an Eastern phenomenon? In the West there is a growing body of evidence to suggest that it is not. I set out to find some of the leading Western researchers in the field of reincarnation, to hear their views and to check the similarities and differences between their approach and that of the Tibetan lamas.

One of the most interesting people I came across was Dr Roger Woolger, a British Jungian analyst, lecturer on cultural psychology and past-life therapist, who examines the impact of past lives on people's present existences. With his degrees from Oxford and London Universities, his accreditation from the C. G. Jung Institute in Zurich and his best-selling book *Other Lives, Other Selves* he has successfully combined an 'establishment' background with ground-breaking work in the field of psychotherapy.

Dr Woolger believes that past-life memories can radically affect the quality of life that we experience today. As such he spends much of his year holding five-day workshops in Europe and North America on past-life and regression therapy. In the five or so years that he has been following this theme, hundreds if not thousands of Westerners have delivered themselves into his hands, willing to delve into the darkest recesses of their minds to seek the reason for their anxieties, phobias, failures and unhappiness. The success of Dr Woolger's approach was, I thought, proof that Westerners are not only ready to accept the idea of past lives, but are willing to try them out experientially. According to Dr Woolger, it makes sense. I spoke to him in his home in upstate New York where he lives with his wife and three daughters.

'People are coming because they've tried other sorts of psychotherapy and they have a feeling there is something more going on than just childhood stuff. They've usually looked at all the usual "answers" to their problem, but strange images and funny feelings keep coming up that don't quite connect. They've usually read my book and heard me lecture and they want to give it a try. At some level they're open to it. Occasionally I get someone who doesn't know I do past-life work and comes for psychotherapy, and in the fourth or fifth session I might suggest we go a bit deeper,' he said.

Dr Woolger works mainly in small groups and occasionally on an individual basis, using a version of Freud's classic 'free association' technique to draw forth the memories of a previous life.

'I use highly charged phrases to provoke an inner psychodrama of imagery,' he said. 'For example, I get someone to repeat a phrase like "I'm never going to see him again", or "They're coming to get me", or "Nobody cares about me", or "I've done something terrible." These are very, very simple phrases, but they act like a fish hook for the unconscious and they bring up personal stories very quickly.'

The phrases he chooses, he said, are drawn from an earlier lengthy private interview, in which he uses his psychoanalytical training to elicit patterns that are running through the client's life.

'I talk to the person in depth, to understand their life patterns and issues, listening, as a therapist, for specific themes. It's how an astrologer would look at someone's chart and say "This person has an issue around power, or abandonment, or health and their body." The astrologer would tune in from the horoscope. I tune in from an interview.'

In practice, the dramas that unfold in Dr Woolger's therapy rooms are extraordinary, moving and profound. And, more

significantly, they often explain otherwise enigmatic and curious problems that have afflicted a person's life. He gave some
examples.

'One lady came to see me who was herself a practising
psychoanalyst, very respectably trained, who had had about
ten years of analysis. There was one issue she couldn't get to,
which was stage fright. She was born with a beautiful voice,
and her family encouraged her to take singing lessons but
she was never able to perform in concerts at school because
she was too terrified. She would sing for the family at home,
but that was all. Singing was somehow associated with terror
and shame for her, and she could never explain it. No one
had ridiculed her in her childhood – nothing had gone on at
school, because she wouldn't sing at school.

'I regressed her, and the memory came through of an
attractive young Jewish woman working in the kitchens in
a concentration camp. One day she was singing – she had a
good voice – and a camp officer overheard her and ordered
her to perform at the officers' concerts. It was a camp brothel,
basically. She refused at first, and they threatened her. "Sing
for us or you will go to the gas chamber," they said.

'To save her own life she agreed to sing. That gave her more
exposure with the other officers, and she became very popular
as a prostitute with them. The shame was so devastating that
finally she could take it no longer and she hanged herself. That
was why, in this life, she could never sing in public. She was
still carrying the trauma and shame from a past life.'

It was indeed a fascinating story, and one which made
instant sense to the woman herself. Dr Woolger then gave
me another illuminating example of his work.

'There was a woman who had assiduously avoided marriage
and who then discovered cysts in both of her breasts. When
I regressed her, she found herself in an industrial city in the
North of England in the early 1880s. She was a young woman
sitting against a wall, slowly dying of starvation, with a baby
futilely trying to suckle from her. The full extent of her
bitterness and despair dawned upon her in her present life. "I

don't have anything to give. I'm disgusted with myself and my breasts," she said. She was able to see that at a deep emotional level she had rejected herself as a nurturing mother, and the negative thought that went with this also contributed to her being rejected by men,' he said.

Roger has literally thousands of intriguing case histories. But what interested me particularly was that they seemed to demonstrate precisely what Lama Yeshe and Lama Zopa had said, albeit in a Western psychotherapeutic context: that our mind is a depository for all that we have done, said and thought, and that we carry over the contents of our consciousness, be they happy or sad, into lifetimes which may be immediate or a long way hence. It also reinforced the Buddhist view that we, rather than any external God, are the authors of our own lives. In the light of the stories that Roger Woolger told me, this was not necessarily a comforting thought.

One of the most fascinating aspects of Roger's work is that his clients do not merely see their past lives mentally – they physically relive them as well. This makes his work both dramatic and plausible, because as the lamas know, what is felt is immediately more authentic and real than what is just thought.

'The client doesn't lie back with his or her eyes closed, passively recounting an inner vision. They actually live it out, experiencing the event with all its drama, excitement or trauma, as if it were happening now! They can go through contortions, convulsions, heavings and thrashings. One client may clutch his chest in apparent pain as he recounts a sword wound, another may become rigidly fixed with his arms above his head as he remembers being tied to a post during torture,' said Roger.

As it was not possible for me to witness a session of this kind, he gave me a condensed transcript of a past-life regression to illustrate exactly what he was talking about. It made riveting reading.

Mike was a social worker who suffered terrible panic

attacks every time he had to make any kind of presentation to his colleagues at meetings. About an hour beforehand he would get uncontrollably nervous, his chest would get very tight, his breathing became contricted, his palms would sweat and he would experience severe heart palpitations. He had experienced these reactions since childhood, whenever he was faced with having to do anything in public.

RW: So what does it feel like every time you go into one of your staff meetings?

Mike: Terrible panic. I feel like I'm going to die. [*Touches his chest.*] Everything feels like it's going to shut down. I can feel my heart beating like crazy when I talk about it now.

RW: So what thoughts go with this? You're clearly in a huge conflict.

Mike: I've got to do it, but I don't want to do it. Oh, my God! How do I get out of it? [*His stomach seems to be tensing up and his arms becoming rigid.*]

RW: What does your stomach want to say?

Mike: I don't want to do it. How do I get out of this? Oh, God! My chest is all tight and my stomach feels like it's going to drop out.

RW: Stay with the feelings and what your stomach wants to say, and just follow it.

Mike: I don't want to. I want to be left alone. Please don't make me! No, not in front of them all! I'm trapped. I can't get out of it. [*He's noticeably writhing from side to side now.*]

RW: Let yourself go into any other life story that these words apply to.

Mike: I get a church. And a crowd. Yes, lots of people. Oh no! I don't want to. Don't make me!

RW: Say that to them, not to me. Stay with the images and your body.

Mike: It's terrible, I'm afraid. I'm not going to show my fear. They're making me go there. Oh help! My hand and neck! They're really hurting.

RW: What seems to be happening to you?

Mike: They've got my wrists bound behind me. Something touching my face. I can't see. Now it's my neck. Oh help! They're going to hang me!

RW: I want you to go all the way through it until it's over. The pain will pass but it needs to be released. Keep saying exactly what you feel as it happens.

The report continued:

Mike's breathing now became intense as he lay writhing on the mattress. He reported tingling in his hands and feet and increasing panic in his stomach. His struggle increased until the end. He was obviously fighting the execution all the way . . .

Finally his body went limp as he reached the moment of the past-life death. He wept, his chest heaving: 'There was nothing I could do,' he said. There was more release and opening in his chest. His breathing expanded considerably when the trauma was past . . .

We took as long as he needed for the energy release to be complete and for all the feelings to be expressed and verbalized. Then we went back to the events that led up to the hanging. Mike remembered himself as a youth who had robbed a man and then, in a tussle, killed him. He was caught by the villagers and brought to trial, where he was condemned to death by hanging.

Mike remembered his jail cell, his huge public humiliation, and above all the sense of powerlessness that sat in his chest and stomach in the last hours before he was taken to the scaffold. Needless to say, as an adolescent in this story his life force was very strong, which was mirrored in his physical resistance to dying. I encouraged him physically to express all aspects of the struggle.

The remainder of our work consisted in helping him disassociate the old trauma from its current life parallels. I suggested affirmations such as 'I am fully in charge. I am

46

proud of my work. There is nothing to be ashamed of any longer.'

Reading this case history and hearing about the others I was struck by the sheer weight of tragedy that Roger Woolger's clients seemed to be carrying around with them from previous lives. It was uncomfortably similar to what Lama Yeshe and Lama Zopa had told us in Kopan – that our lives on the wheel of birth and death are marked by suffering.

Happily, Mike's story turned out well. In later sessions with Roger he reported that the panic feelings before meetings had almost completely disappeared and that he felt a sense of greatly increased vitality and power in his life in general. Roger believed that the trapped and humiliated adolescent in him had been freed and was now contributing energy to his life instead of draining it.

Not surprisingly many people, professional and lay alike, are alarmed at the kind of work that Roger and other past-life therapists are doing. Delving back into one's mind to unearth traumas, they say, is dangerous. How does he answer his critics' accusations?

'To the inexperienced, violent physical release can appear distressing, even dangerous – but it is a commonplace, even essential part of past-life therapy. More and more therapists are finding that all kinds of behavioural problems and complexes have traumatic underlays from past lives which are plainly physical as well as emotional,' he replies.

'I am working from the notion that when you go back to the original events which created the trauma, phobia, anxiety, rage, guilt or whatever, and relive it, you get some distance from it, some detachment, and hopefully you're freed from it. The principle is summed up by the Delphic Oracle: "That which wounds also heals."

'My approach derives partially from shell-shock work done in the two world wars. They found that the only way to relieve shell-shock was to give a drug, sodium pentathol, or to use hypnosis to regress people back to the horrors of the battlefield. They could then release their hysteria, their screaming and terror, and let it go. The work I'm doing is about letting go of old stuff.'

He continued: 'There's an alchemists' saying: "The gateway to peace is exceedingly narrow, and no one may enter except through the agony of his own soul." I believe that. Even in the Christian tradition there is the "dark night of the soul" and the Garden of Gethsemane. A certain amount of suffering is necessary in order to become whole.

'But we do pass through, we go to the other side. Of course, people are terrified of being stuck in it, because for many lifetimes we *have* been stuck in it and we didn't escape. We died horribly, we died in pain, we died resentful – and we don't want to repeat that.

'What I say to people when they are going through a past-life trauma is that these are only memories – only traces. They're like old radio programmes out on the airwaves which they have picked up and are playing through. They are not that person today. I tell them they need to let them go and clean out the channels.'

Roger Woolger is neither a lama nor a mystic but a Western psychotherapist, interested not in eternal verities but simply in helping people to get better. I asked him outright if he believed in past lives.

'I believe in past lives like I believe in dreams,' he answered. 'They are phenomena of the psyche that we call the unconscious. I call it the unconscious because I've been trained in the psychoanalytic tradition. Anything we don't understand we put in that basket!

'What has been happening since the 1840s is that Western psychotherapists have been broadening their concept of what the unconscious is, and what it contains,' he continued. 'In fact, Freud's version of the unconscious is a very narrow one. He restricts the definition to personal memories. Already in the nineteenth century Romantic philosophers were talking of the unconscious as containing the whole of humanity. This is what Jung picked up on. The fact is that we can alter our states of consciousness through meditation, hypnosis and drugs – if you want to use them. We can go anywhere in psychic space. We can go to underworlds and overworlds and other realities, other dimensions. We can also go into what we call "the past". What I would say is that the unconscious is just a new word for multi-dimensional reality.

'The point is,' he said, 'we have access to it. We thought we had lost touch with it. We are coming full circle, back to the experiences that had got lost in the West.

'I'm taking the view that most neuroses arise from unfinished traumas that have been repressed. And I'm extending that idea backwards in time – whatever that is – to let the unconscious tell these other stories which seem to be from other lifetimes,' he added.

In the light of this modern, Western, psychotherapeutic work I wondered whether Roger's clients are in in fact remembering past lives or whether they are not merely clothing their problems in images which render them more understandable and therefore acceptable.

'It may well be,' Roger replied. 'It is one possibility. The unconscious is very creative, so maybe it's re-creating history, or pulling on the stories in the collective unconscious that don't belong to the individual. It's a mystery how that happens – we simply don't know.

'Actually I'm not interested in whether the stories are true or not. They are true for the experiencer, and that's what matters to me – psychological truth,' Roger answered emphatically. 'What I am convinced of, however, is that it is not the conscious ego that produces these stories. They come with such spontaneity. Often the person experiencing them is totally surprised. "Where did that come from?" they say. They might dimly recognize a feature of their recall and say something like "That part of France always upset me", or "I've always been fascinated by Aborigines . . . or North American Indians", but the details of the stories are usually quite extraordinary. Where do they come from?

'We know the unconscious can confabulate – but it's a

chicken-and-egg situation. Are the stories created, or are they memories? You can go round in circles on that one!'

His point was a good one. If the definitions and explanations of what is really happening in past-life therapy are more vague than the strict guidelines of Tibetan Buddhism, the actual material being produced is not. The client delving back into the past actually experiences with vivid individuality (not some kind of mass consciousness) the events produced.

Have Roger's clients ever relived being in another form or in some other non-human dimension, as the Buddhists say is possible? I enquired.

'It happens occasionally. We have UFO abductions, people living on Venus, people living on other planetary systems. I don't always know what to make of them, but I accept they are of other realities. As I said, you can go to any reality at all. It's hard to know whether they are in fact past lives or what you might call "astral travelling",' he said.

'What about past lives as animals?' I asked.

'I have had people remembering mostly things like wolves or dogs, occasionally birds, sometimes horses. Rarely insects or cold-blooded animals. It's usually mammals if it comes up at all,' he answered.

'It seems that spirit, when it is disembodied, can go into an animal body. I'm not sure if that's reincarnation in an animal or whether it's a spirit taking over a living animal. We've learnt a lot about spirit in this work. It seems that once you're out of the body after death, you can stay on the earth plane or you can go to other planes. In some cases people have had such a terrible time in the human body that they're uncertain whether they want to come back in the human body again. To get a little confidence they'll take on an animal body.

'The metaphysics of this stuff are very tricky. You've got to define what is a spirit, what is a soul, what is a body, what is a subtle body – that energetic form which is less gross than our flesh and blood body. No one really agrees on any of that,' he said.

'Were those experiences as animals pleasant, or not?' I pressed.

'It varies. Sometimes they can be quite pleasant. But what you find with, say, wolves, or dogs, is that the same theme that was lived as a human being tends to get relived in a different way as the animal. Suppose you have a human theme of being rejected, an outsider. So you might come back as a wolf and find you're the one that the pack rejects,' he said.

Was this not another way of saying that no one can escape their karma?

Roger agreed, although in his Western terminology he preferred to call it 'unfinished business'. 'I call it the residues of previous lifetimes that are reimprinted in the subtle bodies of subsequent incarnate beings,' he said.

And would he agree with the lamas and the other Eastern beliefs that we have had not just one or two previous lifetimes, but umpteen?

'Jung used to say that everybody carries within him or her an eighty-thousand-year-old being. That is the knowledge of humanity that he or she carries. He called it the Ancestral Memory. There is no question that we have access to it.'

It was an answer befitting a person trained in the recent Western psychoanalytical tradition. The basic premise was the same, that our unconscious, or our subsubconscious, carries imprints of lives far beyond the one in which we are presently engaged. But whereas the Tibetan Buddhism that I had been taught stated specifically that it was our *own* previous actions of body, speech and mind that karmically created our present condition, the Jungian tradition that Roger was quoting seemed to be saying that we are individually linked to the mass consciousness of the whole of humanity – that we picked up and lived out events and deeds that were not necessarily of our own making.

Roger agreed that this was so, up to a point. 'Some of the experiences of humanity bother us, but not all of them. I don't think we have to carry all of humanity,' he added. 'It's like a horoscope. You don't have planets in every house. Everyone has a different chunk to work on in each incarnation. In the end it's all connected to the larger picture.'

The plot of an already complex story was getting thicker – although I felt I could detect the resonances of similarity between the Eastern and Western interpretations of reincarnation. The most striking of these was that most noble of all ideas – that we are linked to a 'larger picture' and therefore the suffering of one, the crime of one, the shame and disgrace of one, diminishes the whole. Conversely, the noblest, finest, loftiest deed of any individual augments the well-being of us all.

That, distilled, was the entire Tibetan Buddhist message: that each individual strives for Enlightenment – that state of being a fully awake, fully aware, fully *conscious* individual – purely for the sake of all sentient beings. That Western thinkers were coming up with approximately the same notion – albeit in a vastly different form – was indeed exciting.

Did Roger, from his perspective and his methods, believe that it was possible for us to free ourselves from the 'memories' of the past – collectively or otherwise? His answer was surprisingly Buddhist.

'Only by becoming conscious, only by looking at our patterns – not just the healthy ones, but the unhealthy ones, the ones we tend to repress. Only by bringing them to consciousness can we become free. That's what the psychoanalysts, the Jungians say,' he said. 'Of course,' he conceded, 'it is painful to go back, live through and acknowledge the unhealthy patterns we are carrying.'

While Roger was talking, it struck me that his work gave him a rare position to view the death process objectively, while it was being played out by his clients. His testimony could provide another window on that most mysterious event of all – one that previously only mystics, mediums and those who have had near death experiences have described.

'A typical peaceful death,' he told me, 'will be reported like: "I'm old and worn out, I'm lying on my bed and I know it's time to go." Then they'll say: "I'm floating above my body and

I can see my family there and they are all crying. I'm sad, but I'm ready to leave." And then they typically find themselves floating upwards to other levels.

'Or the death will be very sudden, such as those on a battlefield. They'll say: "I've got a sharp pain in my back. I'm not there any more." If you were shot in the back, or died in your sleep, you may be carrying the unfinished fears that went with the sudden death. Once you make them conscious you can let them go.

'A lot of people are angry because they've died – many young men were killed in battles they didn't want to fight. They died very angry,' he continued. 'I think that is behind a lot of adolescent aggression – getting drunk, getting into car crashes, that sort of thing. I've met many, many clients who have said that up to the age of eighteen their life was a whirlwind, rushing around, as though they did not have much longer to live.

'I have witnessed long, agonizing deaths too – people undergoing torture, or dying in childbirth.

'Whatever the death, my technique is always to move through until it's over. And when it is over, always, no matter how violent or difficult the death, there is always a sense of closure. It is over, finished. Therapeutically, that is extremely important. It is how we let go of these patterns, these memories, when we know consciously they are over.'

What did he think it was that travels from life to life, that recalls these events from another time?

'I would say it was a bundle of memories held together by common themes. There is possibly some higher principle that holds it together, which you could call a higher self. I'm not sure it's an individual soul in the sense that it's "my" past-life memories,' he said.

That much, at least, was coming close to the Tibetan viewpoint – that there is no solid, inherently existing 'self'; no fixed 'I' and 'my'; no fixed, unchanging 'self' that went from life to life. But can such deeply engrained memories be erased so easily? Can we get rid of our karma that quickly?

'In some cases, yes – but not all,' replied Roger. 'In some cases there's an instant release of feeling – they've let it go. Those people only need two or three sessions. Other memories might take longer. We might take five or ten sessions and there might be a chain of different lifetimes that need to be experienced and expressed. You get chains of lives, particularly around guilt, where there's a convoluted "I did something wrong here, I get punished there, and I come back feeling inadequate and unworthy, and then I compound my guilt." These types of cases are rather difficult to work through. They don't go away immediately. The soul has to experience some sort of atonement, reconciliation, some kind of forgiveness.

'In these cases I put the person through the death experience and talk to spirit figures on the other side to see if there is any possibility of forgiveness. Sometimes there is, sometimes there isn't,' he said.

It would be nice to think that we could eliminate our sorrows by engaging in therapy. And maybe we can – to some extent. But when we've got rid of our fear of relationships, our terror of standing before a crowd, our fear of saying what we feel, or whatever our number one hang-up is, will we find real happiness – true, everlasting peace and happiness? That is the big question that Buddhism addresses. The lamas say it's not that easy.

The quest for total happiness, the ultimate human pursuit, is, they say, a long and arduous journey taking countless eons to achieve! Can the West produce the remedy in a course of ten sessions?

4

JETSUNMA

The journey to Poolesville, Maryland from New York had taken almost four hours. First one of those silver cigar-shaped trains from Penn Station in downtown Manhattan to Washington, DC. Then a modern automatic train to Poolesville, green and lush, in the wealthy outskirts of the nation's capital. I had had much time to ponder.

I recalled how, several years previously, I had read in a newspaper about a woman who had been recognized as a Tibetan tulku and who had run prayer vigils for world peace. That was the sum total of all I knew. Somehow this small snippet of information had lodged in the outskirts of my brain, to be called up when the notion of this book appeared. Now, on the train rattling down the eastern seaboard of the United States, the idea of meeting a woman Western tulku beckoned alluringly. This, after all, was a rare commodity indeed: a female who had been granted the highest spiritual accolade and authority within the overtly masculine world of Tibetan Buddhism. And a Westerner at that. Tracking her down, however, had not been easy. I had not been able to remember her name, and since her official enthronement in 1988 she had kept a very low profile. Through various Tibetan contacts in the USA I finally found her. Her name was Jetsunma Ahkon Norbu Lhamo, and she had a centre just outside Washington.

Over the seventeen years I had been visiting Tibetan Buddhist centres I can honestly say I had seen nothing like the one that was about to greet my eyes. It glistened in the sunlight, a grand, two-storeyed white house fronted by six vast white pillars, looking for all the world like an exclusive country club. I reached this imposing edifice by means of a winding drive flanked with rows of tall flagpoles, immaculately manicured lawns and flower beds. Glancing up to the roof, I saw the first sign of the place's true identity – two golden deer supporting a golden dharma wheel, the national emblem of Tibet. And there, written large on a sign near the entrance, was the equally foreign name: Kunzang Odsal Palyul Changchub Choling. Since its English translation was even more of a mouthful – the Fully Awakened Glorious Dharma Continent of Absolute Clear Light – it was called by its inmates simply 'KPC'.

If the exterior was impressive, the inside was breathtaking. A large central staircase swept up from the central hall to the upstairs rooms, and the whole place was carpeted wall-to-wall in beige. But this paled into ordinariness when I entered the two gompas, without doubt the most beautiful shrine rooms I had ever seen. They were crystal palaces – around the walls was an extraordinary array of huge crystals, strategically placed on plinths and individually lit, like museum pieces. It was, I was told later, the biggest crystal collection outside the Smithsonian Institution in Washington.

The first gompa, where the teachings and ceremonies take place, was hung with royal blue and gold curtains and furnished with fine chairs for those who could not sit cross-legged on the floor. The throne for the teacher stood under a canopy of red, gold and royal blue. In the middle of the room was a huge mandala, surrounded by golden stupas at the base. Against one wall was a statue of Padma Sambhava, the founder of Buddhism in Tibet, and in front of it was the biggest solid round crystal of all. The effect was extraordinary – a cross between a sumptuously exotic Western drawing room and a magic Eastern temple. It occurred to me that no man in Tibetan Buddhism would ever have had the courage to produce such a place of worship, let alone envisaged the concept. It managed to break all bounds of convention, and yet remain unmistakably a gompa of Tibetan Buddhism.

The second gompa was even more fabulous. This was the prayer room, lit by candles, where the twenty-four-hour vigil for world peace still goes on. In the semi-light I picked out yet more gigantic crystals, individually glowing, and the impressive sight of a wall lined with 108 small Buddha statues standing neatly row upon row, like sentinels watching over the holy activity taking place before them. I had seen such sights in Tibet, where entire walls are painted with thousands of Buddhas turning black with the accumulated grease of millions of burning butter lamps – but nothing could match the pristine splendour that Jetsunma had created here in the Poolesville countryside. Turning round to view another wall, I saw an equally amazing spectacle – a display of twenty-one golden statues of Tara, the female aspect of the enlightened mind which represents fast, effective action; they stood in tiers, like some beautiful female spiritual court. It seemed an accolade particularly appropriate here. With a solitary monk sitting on his cushion sending out thoughts for universal harmony and compassion, and the taped voice of Jetsunma herself crying out her haunting invocation for the Buddha to be present, the room vibrated with spiritual power.

Who *was* the woman who had created all this? Jetsunma Ahkon Norbu Lhamo walked into the upstairs sitting room emanating warmth, a discernible kindliness, a bubbling vivacity and, it has to be said, in appearance at least, a middle-of-the-road American ordinariness. She was dressed in a straight-cut beige skirt and top and was wearing make-up and fashionable dangly earrings. Her fingernails were long and painted, her dark brown curly hair was shoulder-length and wild. She was tall, rounded and in her early forties. Nothing gave away her unique status except for the mala – a string of prayer beads – which she played with constantly in her hands; that and the fact that, with her dark, slightly almond-shaped eyes, her slightly down-turned mouth and the general shape of her face, she had a distinctly Tibetan look about her.

I learned that she was, in fact, a walking example of curious contradictions. In the modern Western way she had been married and divorced, more than once. She was the mother of three children – two sons, now in their twenties, and an adopted girl aged five. She lived in a house behind the centre where she cooked, scoured mail order catalogues for clothes (one of her passions), and looked after her husband and family just like millions of American women all over the country.

And yet in the ancient Eastern way, she carried the name 'Jetsunma' – a title more honorific even than 'Rinpoche', the recognition bestowed on male reincarnates. Here before me, in her make-up and high heels, was a woman who had been hailed as a 'Sublime Incarnation', no less. Here was a woman who, it was said, had achieved the spiritual mastery from which she could be reborn in any form she chose and teach directly from her own memory, without any formal training. It was a rare accomplishment indeed. Unlike the other tulkus I had met, Tibetan and Western alike, Jetsunma Ahkon Norbu Lhamo had not been discovered at an early age, nor taken into any Tibetan monastery to bring forth her potential. She had developed it entirely by herself, secretly and alone in the middle of America without help from anyone. The testimony of what she had achieved was there for all to see: the magnificent centre with its beautiful grounds, its exquisite meditation rooms, and the thriving community of followers she had gathered around her. This was clearly one very special lady indeed.

I was fortunate to see her. She had been engaged in a long retreat and was also suffering from flu – yet she agreed to break her silence to talk with me. I was eager to hear this American dakini's tale.

'I'm really just a girl from Brooklyn,' she began, eyes twinkling with humour. In fact there was little in her background to laugh about. She came from a poor family beset with problems. There was alcoholism, violence and abuse, which she was reluctant to say much about except that she was advised by the police to leave home when she was seventeen. 'It was a *very* difficult situation, *very* difficult,' she said quietly. 'As soon as I was able to stand on my own two feet I left. But I did all right. I managed pretty well,' she added, wanting to make light of what was obviously a horrendous childhood.

Her mother was a Jewish grocery store cashier, her step-father an Italian truck driver who drank too much. Both beat the kids. 'It was a very mixed religious household with quite a lot of tension surrounding belief. It's a strange history. My mother, who was Dutch, converted to Judaism when she married my father but never really practised it – instead she stayed with the Dutch Reform Church. She was what we call a "lox and bagels" Jew – someone who didn't really know what was going on in Judaism other than the accent!' Jetsunma said with a deep, throaty laugh.

'I didn't know my real father, but my stepfather was Catholic. There was a real battle in my house as to how the children should be raised. When my stepfather was winning I was Catholic, which meant I was baptised a Catholic and went to a Catholic school where I was taught catechism and the rest. When my mother was winning, or when she could absolutely stand no more of the nuns, she would take me out of catechism and put me into the Dutch Reform Church.'

It seemed to me in the light of what was to follow that her background, hard though it was, probably helped shape her destiny. The violence in her home must have honed her sensibilities to the suffering of the world, both mental and physical, while her Judaeo-Christian schooling would have given her a first-hand knowledge of the very roots of our Western civilization – an invaluable asset when teaching the principles of a very different belief. Jetsunma would know from personal experience the background of most of her audience.

She was a naturally spiritual child, she continued, with a reverence for Jesus which abides to this day. 'I feel an enormous devotion for him. I think he is one of the greatest bodhisattvas of the world,' she said. But she also had an inexplicable attraction to Buddha statues. 'I used to buy them all the time and either give them to my mother or keep them for myself. I remember when I went through my hippy phase I had my room decorated in psychedelic Buddhist posters and had a Buddhist altar. I had an affinity to it. I liked the simplicity. I didn't know anything about Buddhism, to tell you the truth, but there was something about it that felt normal.' She also remembers having beatific visions at the age of ten on her top bunk. And she had prayers that were all her own.

In spite of her innate spirituality she found nothing in either churches or synagogues to attract her. 'I didn't like the way religion was practised in our country,' she said. 'It seemed like a vapid experience. People did not seem to pick up any clues from it as to how to live their lives. I don't ever remember, for instance, being told to care for all sentient beings. I was told to be a good girl, a nice girl, which boiled down to morality. We all knew what good and nice girls didn't do!' she said.

'Certainly in my family I noticed that those same parents who could go to church and do all the right things could come home and beat the stew out of their kids, in the same day! To my mind there was something desperately wrong with that – especially when I was the one getting the stew beaten out of me. For a while I got really angry with "religion" and rebelled against it.'

One thing is sure. In this very eclectic religious and racial background that shaped Jetsunma's early life, there was absolutely no hint of the Tibetan Buddhism which was to emerge so brightly, of its own accord, later in her life. No secret influence, no teachings could be discerned that would explain the emergence of the pure Buddhist philosophy that was to spring automatically from her lips.

'There was no one who put me in touch with Buddhism. Not at all. The only thing that could have connected me, but didn't, was that my mother took me to Coney Island and a palm-reader there told me I was an old Tibetan. That was all. I had no idea about Tibet. Not a clue. When I thought about Tibetans I thought of smelly old men on rugs!'

When she ran away from home on the advice of the police

she headed for Florida, where she met a man and married him. She had a baby and they moved to an isolated farm in North Carolina. That was when Jetsunma's spiritual story began. Finally away from the hubbub of city life and the distress of her own family situation, the greatness that was lying within her began to evolve. Without any particular emotion or even interest in her voice, she explained the extraordinary series of events that followed.

'I started to have a series of dreams – I've had odd dreams all my life. And in these dreams I would be told what to do. A succession of very strange things happened.

'Most of these dreams told me to look for a sign. The first one involved meeting an old woman, she was like a witch in a turreted castle. This woman placed a circle on my forehead and said, "This is who you are, now you have to commence." Three days later a friend of mine asked me to go with her to this woman who did astrological charts, which interestingly are drawn in a circle. We thought it would be a bit of a lark, and so we went. This woman opened the door and, as surely as I'm sitting here, she was exactly the same as the woman in my dream. She had the same face and was wearing the same clothes. I remember breaking out in a sweat!

'She was really old, but somehow I was very attracted to her. I remember looking at her and thinking she was beautiful. Anyway, she said she wanted to do my chart. After a while she came back and said, 'My dear, I have nothing to say to you. Your whole life is laid out, you don't need any advice from anybody.' I think she was very skilful because she didn't crystallize anything – she let it stay fluid.

'Three days later I had another dream which showed me the farm where I was living, but there were extra cars outside the porch. A thunderstorm blew in, and the sky was unusually green. Well, three days after this dream – it all seemed to be happening in three-day periods – I'd gone out shopping and come home with some friends in their cars and the thunderstorm happened. In the dream a voice had said, "When you see this, it is time to begin your meditation."'

To say Jetsunma was taken aback would be an under-statement. She was just nineteen years old at the time, and wondered why these things were happening to a poor 'girl from Brooklyn'. Furthermore, she had no knowledge of or training in meditation.

'I went out on to the front porch and looked at the scene to make sure it was exactly like my dream. It was. Then I went back into my bedroom and lay down! I knew that if I prayed for guidance I would get to learn how to meditate, as the dream had instructed. That was the start of my real spiritual training,' she said. It was to be highly individual and quite unorthodox.

'The first thing I was "told" was that I had to make a very deep commitment that everything I did from here on would be a channel for blessings. So I used to do this meditation where I would say things almost as if I were chanting a mantra: "I commit myself to benefiting all beings, my life has no meaning other than the benefit of all beings." Unbeknown to her at the time, she was uttering stock Tibetan Buddhist concepts in stock Tibetan Buddhist jargon. Every day she diligently continued feeling her way along her DIY meditations.

'The picture I had was of being a faucet – the water was in there, and I just had to turn the faucet on, kind of thing. I tried to align myself with the principle of broad-spectrum compassion.'

After she felt she could go no further with this particular meditation she prayed for guidance on what to do next. She had another dream which told her to examine all the probabilities that could come out of her life.

'I used to imagine all these white picket fence scenarios – the typical Western dream,' she continued. 'I did these meditations where I would suppose my husband and I were always happy – like in the commercials where you run laughing towards each other through the wheatfields. And my son would grow up to be a doctor – he'd be wealthy and loving! And I would have other sons and daughters and they would grow up to be successful and happy too. Then

I asked myself: supposing I attained every material dream a woman could have in America, then what?

'I meditated on that. It was turning the mind. I saw that these things, these dreams and hopes, were pointless. Where did it lead? After all this, you die. I began to see that there was no future in these kind of endeavours. Even if I were to be totally happy in this world and invested all my time and money in it, there was ultimately no point. I might get the admiration of my peers, and all the riches I could dream of, then I would die. Then what?'

What she was describing was the basic Buddhist meditation on death and impermanence that I myself had done in Kopan back in 1976.

'I remember meditating on this, holding my son in my arms and thinking how I wanted to protect this little being and feeling I would do anything for him. I remember thinking "I absolutely commit myself to making you safe." And then I realized in my meditation that I couldn't make that commitment. If my son were to become terribly ill and die there would be nothing I could do about it. I couldn't follow him into the after-death experience. I realized I was lying to my baby,' she said.

This relentless scrutiny of her life, the various ways it could go and the inevitable outcome in death was to have a critical impact on her life. From then on she turned her back on worldly pursuits. In Buddhist terms she had achieved renunciation – the lack of fascination with the ups and downs, the dramas and the joys, of mundane existence. It is said that only when you achieve renunciation do you truly step on to the spiritual path, because only then do you stop believing that following the goals of material existence is the way to happiness.

'I left the party at that point,' was how she put it. 'I felt "There's nothing here."' Her meditations then took a quantum leap – right to the heart of mysticism, to the fount of truth.

'In my next dream I was guided to meditate on the question

"If what I have here does not amount to much because it is so finite, then what is there of value?"' Suddenly she found herself contemplating absolute reality, or ultimate truth, the primordial wisdom state and the most profound and difficult subject of all Buddhist meditations.

'I didn't have the words for it but I knew it wasn't like God, the old-man-on-the-throne idea. What I was meditating on was a non-dual, all-pervasive essence – that is, form and formless, united, indistinguishable from one another. I saw that it was the only validity – that and the compassionate activity that was an expression of it.'

What Jetsunma was telling me was, I recognized, quite exceptional. What yogis and scholars in the Tibetan monasteries take years to achieve after long intellectual delving and even longer years of retreat, Jetsunma had arrived at entirely of her own accord. Tucked away on her farm in North Carolina without any guru, any book, any established doctrine or example to follow, she had not only discovered but realized the two essential truths – wisdom and compassion, the two wings of Tibetan Buddhism that are said to fly you all the way to Enlightenment. Without them you can barely get off the ground. It was an amazing feat.

But she didn't stop there. While she continued to meditate on absolute nature and compassion she simultaneously began to offer up her body, part by part.

'This is going to sound very strange,' she said, laughing, 'but I would lie down – I didn't know you were supposed to do all of this sitting up – and I would look down at my feet and say, "OK, here they are, ten toes." And I would really look at my feet and consider all the things that I could do with them – like walk, run, dance, grow toenails. I would really go into all the good things that my feet could do for me. And then I would contemplate what was the ultimate good of these things – no ultimate use at all! Then I would say, "I offer my feet to the absolute nature so that where I am my movement will be that nature."' She would continue in that vein throughout her entire body, staying longer on the parts she felt attached

JETSUNMA

to. 'No one wants to give up their head, for instance. Our head is like the last bastion of our individuality. And I'd pay special attention to my female parts and my hands. You don't want to do without them!'

She didn't know it then, but what she was doing was no less than Chod, another profound Tibetan meditation whereby you relinquish your body to emptiness for the good of all. It is considered the ultimate physical surrender. How she had come across such a strange meditation in the middle of North Carolina, with only a baby and husband for company, adds to the mystery. I asked again, to make sure, if there were any outside influences that could have been directing her.

'We were in Ashville in the seventies and nothing metaphysical was happening there,' she replied. 'Actually there was one thing – a small transcendental meditation centre had started and friends kept urging me to join. But I resisted. It didn't feel as though it was the right place for me. They said I had to have a guru, that I couldn't get anywhere without one, and I replied, "That may be true, but I haven't found my teacher yet and I will know when I do."'

She continued these intense periods of individual meditations over several years. 'I would meditate for hours at a time. Luckily I had a baby who was peaceful and slept a lot, and a husband who was supportive of what I was doing. I am eternally grateful for that. But it was still a householder's retreat. I had a husband, a child and all the chores to do. Even so, I had a much stricter schedule of meditation than I do now.'

The meditations grew in strength and clarity, and when she was around thirty she had a spiritual experience which showed that the time to begin her work had begun. She was reluctant to tell me about it, except to say that she entered a long period of meditation from which she emerged knowing that her personal life had finished and that she had been born solely to be of benefit for others. 'I never said anything to anyone about it. But oddly, after that people started coming to me.'

*   *   *

I spent a couple of days at KPC admiring the grounds and meeting some of Jetsunma's followers. One of them was Wib Middleton, a friendly, open man who was one of Jetsunma's earliest students and is now the chief administrator. I asked him for his impressions of this first female Western tulku as she ventured out on her mission.

'When we met her it was in 1981 and she and her family had moved to Washington. We were really drawn to her. We were a group of seekers, about ten of us, New Age-type people who felt there was a lot more to life and who had an innate sense of wanting to contribute to society. But we didn't have a vehicle for that. We looked around, but a lot of the New Age stuff seemed to be so self-focused and self-centred. When we met her she had a very expanded way of talking about things. She talked about "planetary consciousness and planetary quickness" and "the vibrational zero" which was her word for emptiness. It was really amazing stuff,' he said.

'We went and asked her to teach us, and she said "Sure." So we began meeting in living rooms about once a week. She started teaching us meditational practices and we'd have discussions which she would lead. Looking back, I can see that she was using really skilful means in how she taught – she was addressing the specific needs of people around her,' he said.

'Although she taught confidently, as though from an inner authority, she never made claims for herself in terms of what her abilities were,' he continued. 'She has never done that. In fact, she has always publicly refuted the idea that she has any special qualities at all. She was always very humble. She says things like she is not a very good teacher, that she has no particular abilities. Still, we could see that she had developed certain inner qualities and had crossed certain lines of consciousness,' Wib said.

If Jetsunma's spiritual life was accelerating, her material life was deteriorating quickly. Money and physical comfort were in extremely short supply. She and her family were living in a one-roomed place with crates for furniture. She had steadfastly refused all payment for her meditation classes and was working in the clothing department of a big store while her husband was trying to find a teaching job. When things got really tight, Jetsunma announced that she was thinking of returning to North Carolina where her husband had the chance of a teaching position.

'When we heard that, we went crazy,' said Wib. 'We thought, "This is our teacher, we *need* to keep her around." The group had grown to about a dozen or more. Late one night we dashed over to her place, knocked on her door and said, "Look, here's the deal. We'd like to start formal classes. We'll pay. We'll start an organization, and the organization pays you." She replied, emphatically, that she didn't want to be paid to teach. We said we'd work it out so that it wasn't like that. We'd have an organization with a board of directors and we'd take care of it. And that's what we did. We started formal classes and an organization called the Centre for Discovery and New Life. We had a little logo and a board of directors,' he recalled.

After that the organization grew organically. Soon there were two classes a week, then three. And all the time the teachings that Jetsunma was giving were becoming deeper and deeper.

'Every week it would be more mind-stretching, more amazing than the week before. We would walk in and think, "There is no possible way that the information she is going to give us could get more profound", but it was. She was teaching about the nature of the mind, the void, different subtle bodies. At that stage we were between Western metaphysical language and Eastern concepts. We certainly weren't calling ourselves Buddhists.'

The teachings continued pouring forth out of Jetsunma – week after week. Little did the group know it then, but they were all being prepared for what was to follow. When it happened, they didn't notice it all.

'One of our friends introduced us to a Tibetan called

Kunzang Lama from a monastery in south India,' continued
Wib. 'He came to our centre one rainy night with a lot of
carpets he was trying to sell to raise money for the monastery.
He also had a book of pictures of small Tibetan kids – mostly
young monks who needed clothing, books and food. At this
meeting we decided to take them on as a project. None
of us knew anything about Tibet and we knew very little
even about Buddhism. Our knowledge was restricted to
Vietnamese monks burning themselves – and there was
some confusion with the Hare Krishna movement! It was
the typical American response to somebody else's culture
and religion,' he said, laughing.

Entranced by the pictures of the little monks, they realized
that there was an excellent opportunity to put Jetsunma's
teachings into practice. 'Right from the beginning she had
emphasized compassion, seeing suffering and doing something about it. She said that suffering came about because
we thought of ourselves as "separate". She talked about
"union consciousness" – recognizing that there's one operating principle – and that the one way to understand our own
and everybody else's nature was through love and kindness.
She talked a lot about "stewardship" and "caretakership" of
the earth and all the creatures on it.'

Within two or three weeks of the carpet-seller's visit
they had managed to sponsor seventy-five children back in
south India, and a rewarding correspondence followed. They
learned what the little monks were doing and discovered it
wasn't so different in intention from what they were doing
in Washington. They also learned that the abbot of the
monastery was called His Holiness Padma Norbu Rinpoche,
commonly referred to as Penor Rinpoche, who was the head
of the Palyul sect of Nygma Buddhism.

The tale fast-forwards a year to when the group received a
letter from the carpet-seller saying that Penor Rinpoche was
making his first-ever teaching tour of the United States. He
wanted to visit Washington to meet and thank the people who
had generously sponsored so many of his young monks.

The group was delighted, but had no notion of who or what Penor Rinpoche was nor how to treat him. By this time Jetsunma had moved to a bigger house because they could no longer fit into her living room, but she was still doing everything herself, including all the cleaning, setting out chairs, organizing the coffee and snacks, and of course looking after her family.

Penor Rinpoche arrived in spring 1985. When the group went to Washington Airport to meet him they found a large crowd of Chinese students already waiting to greet their guru. Unknown to the members of the Centre for Discovery and New Life, Penor Rinpoche was an extremely eminent lama with several established centres in Asia. Later they learned that back in Tibet he had been responsible for a hundred thousand monks and nuns situated in over a thousand monasteries. Like all the great Tibetan lamas he had left his homeland in 1959 after the Chinese invasion. Starting with five hundred followers, he arrived in southern India fourteen months later with only twelve: the rest had died on the perilous journey. Undeterred, he took the five acres of land and the elephant that the Indian government offered and, against what seemed insurmountable odds, proceeded to build a monastery that could hold five hundred. When Jetsunma and Wib met him his monastery was crammed to overflowing with 650 monks, all of whom had fled from the continuing persecution in Tibet.

Penor Rinpoche had one burning ambition left in life. Since he was young he had prayed to meet, in this lifetime, the reincarnation of Genyenma Ahkon Lhamo, the female Tibetan yogini who with her brother had founded his lineage, the Palyul sect, back in 1652. Penor Rinpoche was sure she was living on this earth somewhere. He had already met Ahkon Lhamo's brother, a Tibetan who was also teaching in America in Ashland, Oregon. But he knew that female reincarnates were immeasurably harder to track down. Tibetan yoginis, although reaching the same exalted peaks of consciousness as their male counterparts, were generally free spirits who did their meditations alone in caves. There was no system set up for finding them.

None of this was known to the small group of Americans who turned out to meet Penor Rinpoche's plane on that spring day in 1985. What followed next was a scene befitting a Hollywood movie. Jetsunma described it to me in detail.

'We arrived at the airport and there was this huge group of Chinese people who had got wind that he was coming and had arrived with a limousine. They knew who he was. We didn't have a clue. They were all grouped around something or someone I couldn't see, clicking their cameras and carrying on. Now Penor Rinpoche is short, about five foot three inches, and fat. I tower over him. I thought, "Well, I guess he's in there somewhere, but what's happening?" Somehow the sea of Chinese people parted, I saw him, and burst into tears!

'Now I'm not the sort of person who usually does this kind of thing, you understand. I'm a hard-headed lady. I'm from Brooklyn, for heaven's sake!' she joked. 'But I just could not pull myself together. I felt such a ninny. I cried and cried. I just looked at him and thought, "That's my heart . . . That's my mind . . . That's everything."' Her voice was soft. 'How do you feel when you have just seen everything? I just *knew* that was it. That was what I'd been looking for my whole life. And the tears poured down my face.'

I asked her what precisely she meant.

'Padmasambhava, the founder of Buddhism in Tibet, actually said, "I will reappear as your root teacher, the one with whom you have such a relationship that you understand the nature of your own mind. When you meet your teacher you will in some way see your own face, and it will be the face that turns around and moves you. It is the beginning of your awakening."'

She went on to talk a little about the place of the guru in Buddhism. 'The guru is an emanation of enlightened compassion, and that compassion is like a hook or a piece of Velcro,' she explained, slipping into her hallmark mode of putting Eastern concepts into Western terminology. 'Now

Velcro has to have a corresponding piece, otherwise it won't connect – which means that at some time in the past you have already had a relationship with the guru. It is not as though the teacher will know your name, or something like that. But the power, the intention of compassion and loving kindness sets up a vibration, almost like a sound, and students begin responding to that vibration. And the student will be called.

'That sound is so subtle, yet so powerful, that it changes the student's life – like that,' she said, clicking her fingers. At this point I realized she was talking about herself as 'guru' too. 'And it can sustain that change. It can change the world. That sound is the greatest, the most gossamer force there is – bodhicitta, the force of compassion. That's the sound that is being vibrationally cloaked to suit the student's mind,' she explained.

At Washington Airport, however, Jetsunma had no idea that the small, rotund man who was making her weep was her guru; that was to come. Instead she was contemplating how to get him back home and what to give him for lunch. He eventually scrambled into her old car and was driven back to Poolesville, where the group fed him hot dogs and potato crisps on the back porch. For an auspicious meeting it was, like Jetsumna herself, highly irregular.

'We didn't know what to do with him,' she confided. 'We had a barbecue going and were sitting down next to him, being friendly and chatty. I had no idea one doesn't do this. But he seemed really happy to be with us and said he wanted to meet all my students and ask them questions. I was amazed. He added that we could ask him questions too. Now *that* I could understand,' continued Jetsunma.

All day long Penor Rinpoche interviewed all of Jetsunma's students in great depth, probing to find out exactly what she had been teaching them. When eventually Jetsunma herself managed to get some time with Penor Rinpoche, she acknowledged him as the teacher and confessed her 'sin' of teaching without any real qualifications.

'Forgive me, but I did not feel I could sit doing nothing,'

she said. 'But the authority under which I've been teaching
is twofold. First of all, I look around me and see there is
suffering, and I have to do something. The other is that I've
tried my own practices and I know that they work. But I
don't really know *why* these teachings come to my mind.
Can you please tell me where it comes from?'

Penor Rinpoche looked her straight in the eye and broke
the news – at least, part of it. 'In the past you were a great
bodhisattva, a person who works throughout all time to
liberate sentient beings. You have attained your practice to
the degree that in every future lifetime you will not forget it.
You will always know it, it will always come back to you. It
is in your mind and will not be forgotten.' He gave her no
name, no clue as to what kind of bodhisattva she had been.
He just advised her to keep on doing precisely what she was
doing, in the way she was doing it, and confirmed that her
teachings were exactly what her students needed. That was
all. It seemed that no great demands were to be made of her
– until he dropped the bombshell.

'He told me that I had to buy a centre, a real temple, that I
shouldn't be afraid. He said I was going to see several different
places but I had to buy the one with the white pillars in the
front. "You're going to think you can't afford it," he said –
and oh, we can't! – "but you will find a way. Have faith, it
will be all right. Eventually," he added, "you will have places
all over the world."' The last part of the prophecy is still to
come about.

After Penor Rinpoche had left, the group dwelt on all
that had happened and what he had said. Dutifully they
began looking for a property and, sure enough, they found
a beautiful place which would suit their purposes perfectly.
It had white pillars all along the front. But the price was
astronomical. Scraping together whatever money they could,
and taking out a huge mortgage (which now necessitates
many ingenious fund-raising schemes), they bought what is
now KPC and established what over five years has become
the largest ordained Buddhist community in the USA. Every

Sunday over 120 people come here from the surrounding area to hear Jetsunma's teachings.

At this stage Jetsunma still didn't know precisely who she was. That was still to come.

A year after Penor Rinpoche's visit Jetsunma felt the urge to see again the small, round man who had come into her life and touched her so deeply. She decided to go to India, to his monastery in Bylakuppe in Karnataka state. For the girl from Brooklyn who had never set foot outside the USA, landing in Bombay with its chaos, colour and poverty was merely a prelude for the greater revelation that was to follow.

Facing Penor Rinpoche on his own territory, she said she wanted to take the bodhisattva vows. This is the ceremony in which you formally promise to dedicate your life to the well-being of others. She asked if he would give her a spiritual name, as was the custom at such an occasion.

'When the time is right,' replied Penor Rinpoche.

'When will the time be right?' pushed Jetsunma, with typical Western impatience.

'I'll give it to you when the right day comes,' continued Penor Rinpoche.

'When is the right day going to come?' persisted Jetsunma, not giving up.

'When I say so,' retorted Penor Rinpoche firmly.

Jetsunma gave up.

One day, when the moon was in a particular place in the heavens, Penor Rinpoche called her to him and announced: 'Now I am ready to give you your name.'

He then wrote out her spiritual name on a piece of paper, rolled it up into a scroll, put his personal seal on it, then handed it to her with the white katag (scarf) of respect wrapped around it. 'That's your name – Ahkon Lhamo,' he said.

There was no apocalyptic vision, no instant flashback to another time, another place, another body. There wasn't even shock or surprise. Just a sense of intense familiarity.

'I experienced serious *déjà vu*,' was how Jetsunma recalls the occasion. 'I felt a strong connection to that name. I asked him to say it again. It was like milk to my ears.'

Through his translator he then uttered the monumental words: 'I now recognize you as the sister of Kunzang Sherab. Her name was Ahkon Lhamo. In that life she and Kunzang Sherab co-founded the Palyul tradition. I recognize you as her incarnation.'

And in those few simple sentences Penor Rinpoche made sense of the extraordinary life that Jetsunma had etched out for herself and the otherwise inexplicable abilities she possessed. This, at last, was the official explanation of how a woman with no Buddhist training whatsoever, no books on Tibetan Buddhism, no teacher, no outward example to follow, had been driven to enter years of strict meditation by herself and to emerge with not only profound wisdom but also the wish and the ability to help others fulfil their spiritual potential.

Before receiving her bodhisattva vows she had told Penor Rinpoche of her own vow that she was teaching to her students: 'I dedicate myself to the liberation and salvation of all sentient beings. I offer my body, speech and mind in order to accomplish the purpose of all sentient beings. I will return in whatever form necessary, under extraordinary circumstances, to end suffering. Let me be born in times unpredictable, in places unknown, until all sentient beings are liberated from the cycle of death and rebirth.

'Taking no thought for my comfort or safety, precious Buddha make me a pure and perfect instrument by which the end of suffering and death in all forms might be realized. Let me achieve perfect enlightenment for the sake of all beings. And then, by my hand and heart alone, may all beings achieve full enlightenment and perfect liberation.'

Penor Rinpoche had rocked to and fro in unbridled mirth, slapping his thigh in amusement. She had replicated almost exactly the same words that Tibetan lamas spoke. It was another proof of her identity.

He handed her another certificate, authorizing her to teach. 'This is important,' he said. 'People will say you haven't been studying the dharma, that they have never heard of you. They will not understand. With this paper no one will doubt that you are capable of teaching the dharma.'

Penor Rinpoche went on to tell Jetsunma a little about her famous 'predecessor'. The first Ahkon Lhamo was the direct student of Terten Nigyu Dorje, a famous revealer of secret teachings, he said. She was a great dakini and spent decades in retreat, only coming down from her cave to help her brother with the monastery. Otherwise people would go to her to receive healing and teaching.

I asked Jetsunma if she were curious to find out more about Ahkon Lhamo or had any memories of the yogini who had lived in Tibet in 1665 and had inspired a religious order which had survived to this present day.

'I discovered that she was pretty wild,' she replied. 'She stayed up in her cave and looked pretty wretched, with her hair sticking out all over the place,' she said, picking up her own unruly locks. 'She was a crazy yogi type. Some things never change! There was no water in her cave, of course, and she never bathed. Her clothes were rotting on her. But people said that whenever they went to her cave it would smell like perfume. Penor Rinpoche told me that people would give her turquoise, gold and coral, but she would refuse it. She was probably holding out for gifts she could accept, like hair-driers! She was probably waiting for electricity to be put into her cave and she could have central heating!' she joked.

'As for any memories, I don't like to make any fuss about the inner experience I have. I can tell you I have some awareness of it, but it's pretty "Swiss cheesey". I *am* curious. I want to go back to Tibet, to see the cave where she practised. Jaltrul Rinpoche, the reincarnation of Kunzang Sherab who is now in Oregon, said that when he went back to Tibet he remembered a lot. It's as though the airways are clearer there.'

There is at least one concrete link between this latter-day

bodhisattva, the girl from Brooklyn, and the seventeenth-century Tibetan yogini who had helped found a Buddhist lineage. Ahkon Lhamo's skull, or part of it, is still in existence. It bears an unmistakable hallmark of sanctity. In its side is etched the holy syllable 'Ah'.

The story goes like this. When the first Ahkon Lhamo passed away, they prepared a pyre to cremate her and duly put the body on it. When the last vestige of flesh was burnt away the skull rose up in the air in front of hundreds of people and flew about a mile before landing at the Palyul monastery, in front of her brother Kunzang Sherab. This was considered the final ultimate display of Ahkon Lhamo's power and spiritual accomplishments. The great dakini, who was already known for the many miracles she performed, had revealed her true greatness.

The skull became a most treasured relic and was used as a capala, an instrument used in ritual ceremonies for holding nectar. It remained intact until in the mid-twentieth century the invading Chinese hacked to pieces everything of spiritual significance, including the precious capala at the Palyul monastery. A lay person saw a piece of the skull among the rubble and, hiding it in his clothes, took it to safety. It was some years before Penor Rinpoche got word that at least part of the holy relic had survived.

There was a vast gap in time between 1660 and 1949, when the present Jetsunma Ahkon Lhamo was born. I asked her the same question I had asked Tenzin Sherab. What lives did she think she had been living in between?

'I think there were other incarnations, but as Penor Rinpoche told me, they don't keep track of the women. It wasn't because they were prejudiced against women's wisdom. In fact, dakinis are the primordial wisdom beings and are held in very high regard. Generally, though, dakinis were not the lineage holders. They spent their lives in solitude, doing spiritual practices. Penor Rinpoche says, and I feel, that there have been many incarnations.'

But this present one, as the American woman doing it 'her

way' as undoubtedly she always had, was the life that was to capture widespread attention. Jetsunma left the United States as a married woman, mother of two and teacher of New Age metaphysics with a bent for worldwide caring, and returned a recognized tulku, a reincarnate lama. For her students this took some adjustment. While they had been happily following the teachings of a woman whom they treated as their equal, they now had to contend not only with a 'Buddhist' but also with someone whose rank placed her on an entirely different footing. There was protocol to observe, a new language to learn for the same concepts they had learnt, and the mantle of an old and established 'religion' from the East to adopt. Some disciples fell out, but most survived the transition.

Whatever misgivings they might have had about the authenticity of their teacher's new lofty reincarnate status, however, were completely dispelled when Penor Rinpoche came to see them for the second time in 1988. He arrived at Poolesville with twelve monks in attendance and conferred the entire teachings of the great Padma Sambhava to all members of KPC. It was the first time he had ever performed the task, and only the sixth time it has been done this century. It was the biggest endorsement of Jetsunma's qualifications he could give.

He then conducted an official enthronement of Jetsunma Ahkon Lhamo. News of the thirty-nine-year-old woman who had been recognized as the reincarnation of a famous Tibetan yogini reached the media. Newspaper reporters and television crews descended on KPC. 'Meet Ahkon Norbu Lhama, Tibetan Saint,' blazed the front-page headline of the *International Herald Tribune*. 'The Unexpected Incarnation,' cried the *Washington Post*. She appeared in the popular *People* magazine. Leading Japanese and German magazines ran articles on her. This was when my own journalist's antennae, primed for good stories, must have picked up the importance of the event and stored it away for later use.

Sceptics might think that the woman known universally as

Jetsunma Ahkon Lhamo would be revelling in fame and wealth after her debut on the world stage in 1988. Nothing could be further from the truth. She was now steeped in the business of keeping a large centre financially afloat and had become an eminent public figure. This was not what she had bargained for when she embarked on her life purpose of teaching the profound spiritual truths that she had discovered. When I asked her how she enjoyed being a recognized reincarnate lama, the answer was voluble and emphatic.

'I hate it! It's not the life I wanted at all. Oh no! No!' she declared. 'The day I got enthroned was in many ways the day I went to jail. I am really *very* private. If I could build my house with turrets and guards to stand there and say "Go away" when people came up, then I would do that. This recognition has been the bane of my existence. I'm not cut out for it personality-wise. Now I represent the dharma. I love dharma from the depth of my heart, it is my nectar, but I don't want the dharma scene at all. Everywhere I go, people judge the dharma by me, so I often try to go to places where nobody knows who I am. Then I can relax. I could go to different centres all the time now and be well received, but I don't. My life is about compassion. That's all I care about.' It was an honest, heartfelt cry.

When she had been recognized by Penor Rinpoche she had offered to shave her hair and become a nun, but Penor Rinpoche had declined. 'He said I could reach more people as I am. I prefer to be treated normally,' she continued. 'I like to look like a Western woman of my age, to dress normally, to think normally. Before I met Penor Rinpoche I tried to make everything democratic. I thought in terms of "us" forming the meditation group and that the dynamo, the energy that would unite us would be the prayer for the world. I believe in prayer. It was much more democratic – without the attention being on me.

'My best wish, my everyday hope is that I can return to this. In fact, as much as I've been able to turn reponsibility over to others I have done that. I feel that everyone should be strong,' she added.

In the light of these feelings, I wondered why she had adopted the Tibetan Buddhist guise. After all, she was going along very well in her own way, non-aligned to any set religion or path. As a Westerner she had found her truths – ones which bore her own distinct mark – completely of her own accord. Why has she now adopted the mantle of Tibetan Buddhism? Had she, in some way, been hijacked, I asked.

Jetsunma was visibly delighted at such a meaty question. Her eyes lit up and she became more animated.

'Actually the dharma has done a lot for us,' she answered. 'I was having a real problem with my students. I thought my spiritual progress had been a step-by-step affair until a few years ago when I realized I had done some quantum leaps. What I noticed was that I had gone from one place spiritually to another place of power, say from A to M, without knowing it. But my students could not jump from A to M or even A to D. My students needed to go through the steps – A, B, C, D – but I myself had no cognizance of those steps as I'd never done them in this life. I just had spaces. So what dharma gave me was a method.'

She went on to illustrate her point. She tried to teach her students the Chod meditation – the offering up of the various parts of the body to the greater good. They tried, but didn't get the same results. 'Many of them fell asleep!' said Jetsunma. 'I couldn't believe it! I remembered when I did this meditation on my farm it was so alive and poignant that I would cry every time. I'd say to my students, "Well, go back and do it until tears well up in your eyes." And off they'd go and try again, and would come back and say, "I fell asleep." It wasn't happening for them, and I didn't know what to do about it.

'So without the dharma, the technology, I don't think I could have achieved the results that I have,' she said.

Still, in many ways the great edifice that she has created, with all its Tibetan trappings, bemuses her. Sometimes, she says, she looks around at her great building, the large community of ordained nuns and monks that have gathered around her, with nothing less than sheer amazement.

'I wonder how it could have happened. Personality-wise I'm not one for "religion" – I find ritual and dogma exhausting. I also find the protocol confusing. To this day I really don't get the protocol. I wasn't brought up with it!' she confessed.

Her voice went quiet: 'I would rather practise simply, in a cave somewhere. I'd rather be an ordinary person for whom compassion was the central focus of my life. If I had to say I had a religion at all, I'd go right along with the Dalai Lama in saying my religion is compassion. That's all I care about,' she repeated.

'Having said that, however, I know that dharma is the only method that is effective in a world such as we have now. It works! It comes from the mind of Enlightenment and it results in Enlightenment. The seed and the fruit are complicit on the path,' she said, her eyes shining with conviction. 'And so I have to do it.'

As I looked at her and listened to her speak, it seemed as though Jetsunma Ahkhon Lhamo was standing on the bridge between two different cultures, two modes of thinking, two ways of being. She was like a tree whose roots were firmly grounded in the solitary mystical tradition of the East, while her branches were flowering and bearing copious fruit in the West. But for all these curious dichotomies, she was surprisingly clear about her path in this life and where it was leading.

'Here's what I think is going to happen. The ritual and the technology will be practised purely, in my temple at least. The teachings will not be altered one iota. But it will change in as much as Buddhism changed when it went to Burma, Thailand and China. We will develop our own flavour.

'I also think that we will become more comfortable with Buddhism. We are still very uptight and "proper", like new converts. I have met old Tibetan monks who are just as friendly as they can be. They hug you and are very congenial and make no big deal about things. But that's the maturity of a long-established religion. I think that's going to happen to us, but right now we're a bit stiff. We're also infatuated with robes – we collect lamas like notches on a belt. That's ridiculous. You find a teacher who is qualified to ripen your mind and you stick to that teacher and you learn. It's as simple as that.'

My ears pricked up. This was what my own journey into reincarnation was all about.

How much was she herself aware of the great experiment that seemed to be taking place – the transference of the sacred esoteric truths from their secret caves in Tibet to the marketplace of America and the West? And did she know of her own part in this drama? It seemed she did, although she deflected the words from any personal connotation.

'One of the single most important things in terms of Western dharma is the rebirth of tulkus in the West, because even great Tibetan lamas who have come to understand Westerners and their thinking cannot bridge the gap completely. There are things we do that are misinterpreted by the lamas, and vice versa. I've seen it happen over and over again. They can be the greatest teachers, but they often do not know how to put it in ways that we can understand and so we just don't "get" it.

'I think the single most important thing that has to happen, and which I pray for night and day, is more rebirth in the West. I believe it's starting to happen now. I feel we are seeing children who are qualified to teach.'

This was vindication of all my research, all my wanderings. Jetsunma had voiced what I and a few others had suspected, that there was indeed a plan to bring the truths of a living Buddhism to the West, and that the messengers were the new breed of Western tulkus like Lama Osel and herself.

Being with Jetsunma was, I realized, a marvellous opportunity to ask about the workings of reincarnation and karma from a Western perspective. Here, after all, was a woman who spoke in my vernacular, who grasped the problems that the Western mind had with such mysteries, and who apparently had personally mastered its laws to an extremely high degree.

'The Buddha said something like this,' she began. 'It's stupid to go to this psychic, or that psychic, or this great teacher to find out what you were in your past life. All you have to do is look in the mirror. If you are comfortable, it's because in the past you have given comfort to others. If your health is good, in the past you have worked to heal and help others, or saved the lives of others. If you are prosperous, some time in the past you gave to others. If you are lonely, and longing for love and approval, some time in the past you yourself were not kind or loving to others. If you are poor, then you were not generous. If you are not so good-looking, then in the past you were not, with your body, faithful and loyal and virtuous.

'Karma is very simple really. The content of our mind is constantly being displayed as our lives. For every single result that we are experiencing there is a cause, and that cause is in our mind stream,' Jetsunma said.

'Sometimes these things are hard to take in,' she conceded. 'I often get caught myself. I have a friend whom I saw recently, who I consider to be suffering tremendously. I grieve for him in my heart. I somehow feel that he has been victimized. As a child he was abused, and I know that many circumstances made his life very difficult. It's easy to fall into the trap of thinking that we could suffer without cause, that somehow we are victims, that somehow circumstances have occurred to us and that we are "blameless and innocent". That is never the case.

'The problem is,' she continued, 'that we can only see a continuum that started with our birth. And even that we can't remember. But according to the Buddha we have lived many lifetimes, uncountable lifetimes, of every life form since beginningless time. That's when we first considered ourselves "I". The Buddha talks in terms of beginningless time. So our history stretches back to literally time out of mind. And we can't understand how many ingredients we have in our karmic soup right now. At the moment we only see a small slice of our mind's continuum from some stage in this life, and we don't see all the factors which are there. It is this that keeps us from spiritual activity. If we saw the whole picture we would have no problem in diving into dharma, sweaty and wild-eyed,' she said, laughing.

She pondered the question of rebirth and how best to explain it.

'Karma *seems* complicated, but the rules are very simple. It's cause and effect. The biggest factor we have to combat, that we're not even aware of, is our own habitual tendencies. And our habitual tendencies are based on our karma. We have been slothful and lazy over and over again. We have been non-virtuous again and again. It's our habit. A cat is born as a cat because its habit is to be a hunter. That's its habitual tendency. So we have to fight that. We have to surrender to our teachers, surrender to the dharma and say, "I realize I am completely under the control of my habitual tendencies. Give me the way. Tell me what to do so that I can break free."'

Until we gain control of our habitual tendencies, she said, our rebirth is something over which we have absolutely no control. We are totally at the mercy of the habits on our mind streams – thrown into lives which reflect the way we have acted before.

'Until we can consciously reincarnate, we have no control at all over the kind of lives in which we find ourselves after death. People think rebirth is a way out, but to the Buddhist the notion of dying and going to heaven is the happy way out. If we thought that was the end of the yardstick, then it would be "Alleluia!"'

I asked: 'Is the problem that we mistake our present experiences of happiness for the real thing? If we could experience the kind of happiness that the Buddha says exists, if we had a taste of that, then would we still be so caught up in pursuing the goals we do?'

'Exactly,' replied Jetsunma. 'Our minds are so drunk. We

are all junkies. We want a kick, a hit, a buzz. We have this habitual tendency of being reborn because we want the stimulation. Even now, in this lifetime, the reason we don't settle down to do the practice is because we want the stimulation. We have hyper-minds.

'You see, we think that buzz, that hyper-thing, is happiness. But it's like this,' she continued. 'If we could stop our self-absorption for one moment – just one moment, one moment free of desire, free of self-aggrandizement, free of clinging, one moment of pure spaciousness – we'd never want for anything else. If we could have one moment of this it would do the trick.' She paused. 'If we could have one moment of blissful pure awareness, we would understand. The wisdom would be born.'

This was Jetsunma the teacher, the purveyor of spiritual truths. This was the self-taught, self-effacing tulku, trying her best to lead as ordinary a life as possible. But what of the person? Those students who have known her longest are in no doubt about her power and the gifts she has to offer.

'I can say that in the thirteen years that I have known her," says Wib Middleton, 'I've never seen her act in a way other than to help people, to try and end their suffering. It's like her micro-chip is only that. She doesn't have a program for any other behaviour. You look at how she acts and think, "This is remarkable."

'From my point of view she's such a vast incarnation. Tibetan lamas who come here say, "You don't realize who you have got here", and monks will say in awed voices, "She's an emanation of Tara", meaning she's a projection of the Buddha's enlightened action. She also has the ability to oracle, which is a very rare accomplishment. She's quite amazing because of all these attributes that she has demonstrated. The difficulties that we Westerners have is that we see her in an ordinary way. It's more of a challenge for us because she's a woman and not an elderly Tibetan monk. She's a Westerner wearing make-up and dressing like a regular Western woman. Yet the quality of the teachers and teachings that happen here speaks of her purity as a lama.

'She has a house right behind the temple and she lives there with her family. She does a lot of meditating during the day. I think she's always working – not as we know it, as in, say, a job. But there's never a moment when she's not interacting with sentient beings – maybe not physically, but she's always addressing the plight of sentient beings. For instance, she'll be aware of someone miles away who needs to get in touch with her. Or she'll be aware of some danger that's about to happen to someone she knows. To say she is clairvoyant doesn't even describe it. All I can say is that she's constantly working for others. She's always taking care of her flock, to use a Christian term.'

Others who know her describe a multi-talented, multi-faceted woman. They tell of her skill at cooking, her love of vampire movies, her passion for buying clothes (and then giving them away). They say that like every good American she works out, and has been known to take her exercise bicycle and weights away with her on retreat. They say she's spontaneous and modern, can sing and compose music. They say she's extremely funny, with a well-developed sense of humour and a capacity for being quite outrageous. (I got a glimpse of this when I saw a photograph of Jetsunma pinned to the dining room noticeboard. It was a head shot of her winking.)

They talk of her shamanistic nature, and say she visits the Hopi Indians with whom she does prayer work. And, of course, she loves children. This I could see for myself. KPC was the only Tibetan Buddhist centre I had been to which had a play centre and a creche. Jetsunma gathers children around her and teaches them the fundamental truths of the Buddha, such as kindness and the destructive energy of anger and greed. It's one of her favourite things. She calls the children her 'short practitioners', and says they are among her best students.

Nowhere is the extent of her creativity and imgination more

in evidence than in the garden she has designed across the road from the centre. Under her unique vision this piece of land has been transformed into a world of magic and beauty and offered to the general public. Going through a gate you enter a natural mandala, dissected by paths into the Red Garden, Green Garden, Blue Garden and Yellow Garden. It has been laid out so that you walk in a clockwise direction, making a circumambulation of holy objects that Jetsunma has placed in strategic positions. Among the trees you come across silent Buddhas in deep contemplation; in the middle of a grassy glade you discover a huge crystal standing on a stone plinth; in small corners you find Tibetan prayer wheels which you can turn, sending out thousands of prayers in all directions for the benefit of all living beings. In another corner is a stream with irises growing on its banks and a gazebo where you can sit and imbibe the peace.

Walk a little further and you come across the splendid sight of eight tall white stupas, the monuments representing the Buddha's enlightened mind. Each stupa symbolizes one of the eight profound events in the Buddha's life. In the middle of these monuments is a bigger stupa, rising 18 feet high and dedicated to Jetsunma's long life. All the stupas have been filled with prayers and mantras on long, rolled strips of paper, with holy objects, with offerings and precious relics, and then consecrated so that they all vibrate with the power of sanctity. She has plans to build even more stupas including, appropriately, a 75-foot statue of Tara, the mother of all Buddhas.

Wib comments: 'If you drive around Washington you can see about two thousand statues glorifying war – generals sitting on horses, that kind of thing. Here we have living monuments to peace and tolerance, to harmony, pure living, love and compassion. Even if people come just to check them out, we believe they will benefit. If they just see such a powerful object their life is changed, their karmic history is changed, because they've made a connection to the dharma.'

I put my last question to this remarkable woman. 'What do you want to accomplish with this life?' I asked.

'There's so much I want to achieve, it's incredible,' she answered with her characteristic laugh. 'My centre will always be very Buddhist, but I want to offer a sort of wedding cake phenomenon with different layers, and with each layer having a different distance from the centre. There will always be places here for people who are non-Buddhist,' she said. 'I want to build a place for pilgrimage. There's no real places of pilgrimage in this country that Americans can relate to as Buddhists, where they can see and feel the proof of the Buddha's mind. So I would like to create that.

'I want to create a hospice, a place where people who have faith in the dharma can come and die properly, doing spiritual practice, receiving care and not having tubes and things stuck down them.

'I want to grow my school for children, Buddhist and non-Buddhist alike, who wish to learn non-competitiveness, kindness, cooperation, the preciousness of the earth, the law of cause and effect, equanimity and the "vocation of love". We've already begun working on that.

'I want to create a monastery for both monks and nuns where they can live in a community, especially if they had children before becoming ordained. I'd like to help them with that and provide places of retreat for them.

'I'd like to create a tantric college here, so that people can receive higher education in the Buddha's teachings. You see, I'm afraid. The dharma is presently in countries which have shaky political situations. I know nothing is permanent, but America is in a better position than most to maintain a sense of stability, and I believe that if we have a solid centre here the dharma will continue to flourish for some time.'

She had said it. The reason for *her* birth, a tulku's birth, is purely to propagate the truth of the Buddha in as many ways as he or she can, to be of service to others and to help ease the pain and suffering of humanity. Jetsunma Ahkon Lhamo was clearly fulfilling her destiny well.

5

COMING BACK

How does reincarnation work? Who exactly were these Western tulkus? What were they doing here and how, precisely, had they achieved their mastery over reincarnation? I had heard the official version given by lamas according to the strict Tibetan line, but I wanted to hear the Western version. Professor Robert Thurman holds the unique chair of Indo-Tibetan Buddhist studies at Columbia University. He's a brilliantly funny man with a booming voice and a colourful history. For many years he sat at the feet of the great lamas in Dharamsala, home of the Tibetan government-in-exile, and learned to speak and read Tibetan fluently. He then went on to get his doctorate at Harvard. I went to New York to see him, for I reckoned that no one was more qualified to put intricate Eastern concepts into modern Western language. I was not disappointed.

We sat in his office at Tibet House, a centre dedicated to propagating Tibetan culture, where he was currently President, with the roaring New York traffic passing by outside, and spoke about the greatest mysteries on earth. I asked him outright if he actually believed in reincarnation. After all, he was a man of towering intellect, an academic, a scholar. If he thought we could live more than once, and that high masters could be reborn in our midst, then the case for reincarnation had a powerful advocate indeed.

'I certainly believe it,' he exclaimed. 'And I believe there are incarnations in the West, many more than are recognized. First of all we have to distinguish between reincarnation and rebirth. Rebirth is involuntary. It's what happens to all beings who are reborn on the cycle of life – be they humans, animals, hell-realm beings or gods. There they are, depicted on that tanka hanging on the wall,' he said, indicating the brightly coloured Tibetan painting showing the various states into which we can be born. I was familiar with the Wheel of Life, with its graphic illustrations of human beings embracing, giving birth and dying, gruesome figures inflicting horrible tortures, animals wandering across mountain slopes, gods in various sybaritic and quarrelsome poses – all of them contained in a giant wheel held in the jaws of Yama, the Lord of Death.

'In rebirth there's no choice. People are born in these states on impulse as part of a reactive cycle of action and its effects,' he said.

'Reincarnation, on the other hand, is when a being, usually a human being, develops free will in that cycle by being in control of their involuntary actions and impulses. They are therefore able to remain conscious through the transition from death to rebirth, and can choose the precise circumstances of their rebirth. In Mahayana Buddhism that attainment is considered simultaneous with Buddhahood. The word *tulku* in Tibetan is a translation of the Sanskrit word *Nirmanakaya*, which means the emanation body of a Buddha.'

This put the Western men, women and children I had seen in an entirely different light. Had I been talking to actual Buddhas? It was a daunting thought.

'Strictly speaking, no one less than a Buddha can reincarnate,' replied Bob Thurman. 'There are beings, however, who have a strong wish to reincarnate to perform certain tasks, and that intention might push them through their impulses, but it's not totally conscious and not infallible. Now the tulkus are beginning to found here, but I don't think many of the Westerners have any idea that they might actually be Buddhas. They think they just happened to show up here from Tibet,' he chuckled.

He went on to explain Tibet's unique contribution to the world's religious thought. 'Very few people, even those who call themselves Buddhists, like Zen, Theravada Buddhists or Vipassana Buddhists, believe in this notion of incarnation. They are still going on the idea that once you're a Buddha and have reached Enlightenment you're off the chain of life and you're not reborn again. That's why most other Buddhist countries don't accept this tulku business. Even other Mahayanists like Zen or the Pure Land Buddhists in Japan think that once you've achieved the emanation body you're not going to come back and run around town! They think that once or twice in history Buddhas come, but they're not all over the place. This is strange, because all the sutras – the Buddhist canon – have Buddhas emanating everywhere. Dogs and cats can be emanation bodies. Islands, buildings and cities can be emanation bodies. Continents, planets even! If you are a Buddha and you think that people need a planet somewhere, you can create a planet. You can re-create yourself as a planet.

'So to most non-Tibetans the idea that someone who was a lama and ate mo-mos (dumplings) and maybe incarnates as a Spaniard and eats olives, or is incarnated in America and goes to McDonald's, is a completely strange idea. The concept that a Buddha would manifest in the middle of ordinary reality doesn't fit their category. But that's only because they didn't read their sutras well enough and don't understood what a birth emanation body is. The Mahayana scriptural notion of the Nirmanakaya is an extremely magnificent idea,' he said.

The Tibetan Buddhists were different, he continued, because they alone had developed tantra – the esoteric practices whereby the mediator learns to transform the death process into taking the three bodies of a Buddha – the supreme mind or truth body (Dharmakaya), the enjoyment body (Sambhogakaya) and the emanation or form body (Nirmanakaya). The teachings describing the supreme accomplishment that a human being can achieve were by definition not only extremely complex but also exceedingly difficult. I asked Bob Thurman to explain in layperson's language how the great adepts became tulkus – what they actually did to stop being 'reborn' and start 'reincarnating'.

He gave his explanation in the very modern language of computer-speak. 'What the meditator is doing in those five-year retreats is a very technical thing. He's not just sitting there communing with the Great Oneness! He's technically going down, pulling apart his own nervous system to become self-aware from out of his own cells. It's like you are using Word Perfect and you are in the chip. And you're self-aware of being in the chip. The way you have done that is by stabilizing your mind where you can actually go down to the dots and dashes, and you've gone down and down and down even into that.

'In other words the Mahayanist filled with the technical understanding of tantra has become a quantum physicist of inner reality – something like that. What they have done is disidentified from the coarse conceptual and perceptual process. They've gone to the neuronal level, and from inside the neuronal level they've gone to the most subtle neuronal level, or supra-neuronal level, and they've become where it's like the computer is self-consciously aware of itself. The yogi goes right down to below machine language – below the sub-atomic level.

'At that time everything is voluntary. That's why you can control every impulse, especially at death, because you don't become mechanically caught in any coarsely constructed reality. You only *voluntarily* participate in coarsely constructed reality. That's why the death transition is not a problem for you. When you've done this, what you have achieved is not some kind of mystical thing but some very concrete, evolutional thing. It's the highest level of evolution. That's what the Buddha is defined as – the highest level of evolution.'

The explanation was clear, graphic and thoroughly modern. Being somewhat computer-illiterate, however, although I got the picture I could not engage the professor in animated debate. Besides, I was too dazzled by what he had told me. The descriptions of this highest meditation process left me dumb with admiration and awe. What a pinnacle the Tibetans had achieved!

There were many more valuable pieces of information to find out from this highly learned, articulate man. For example, could he give some clarification of how we travel from one existence to another?

'What goes from life to life is the most subtle level of the self. It's called the indestructible drop in tantra, and is also described as the extremely subtle body and mind,' he answered. 'You can actually call it the soul. Now Buddhists stupidly run around saying there is no soul and there is no self, which are ridiculous statements. The Buddha's famous doctrine of selflessness had to do with the metaphysical status of the essence of the person. His whole point was that there is no fixed, rigid self – no absolutely unchanging, independent, sovereign self with your name and serial number engraved on it, which never changes and which is plopped from one existence to another.

'What the Buddha constantly maintained, however, was that there is a relative, constantly living, constantly changing self. He said the person who controls the self is the one who is the master. "Use yourself to conquer yourself," he said. So for the Buddhist the soul is the most subtle level of that self. It is the extremely subtle body and mind that exists in the centre of the heart chakra, like a tiny little drop. At conception the heart chakra (situated at a mid point between the breasts) forms around it. And then at death it unravels as it leaves the body. In itself it is like a constantly self-renovating cell – it is like DNA,' he explained.

Here in plain, modern English was an explanation of the spiritual technology that the Tibetans had to offer, their great gift to the world. Here were no vague definitions, no ecstatic protestations of transcendental experience – this was a description of the very nuts and bolts of the highest spiritual truth, of what we are made of. That vague notion of a soul that I was so familiar with from my Christian upbringing was becoming more plausible by the minute. And I marvelled that the mysteries that the meditators had discovered through direct experience in those far-off Himalayan caves could have

92

been so minutely analysed, described and passed on. Here in the middle of New York was an American professor able to translate such precious information into precise modern language for our education.

'You see,' he went on, 'the impressions are encoded in it just like DNA chains. It's a very complicated thing, like on a subatomic level. Normally a person has no awareness of it, yet it is what constitutes a person's awareness, finally. And the key is, it's a continuum. This indestructible drop has encoded in it a tremendous amount of specific individual information, which is constantly changing. It's being influenced by your experiences of this life. And it's what takes the code of whatever you have developed and learnt in this life into the next life,' he said.

'It seems to me,' I suggested, 'that this spiritual gene that you talk about is a bit like a huge receiving dish, perpetually receptive to any number of decisions we make, habits we form, impressions we have, actions we do and so forth.'

Professor Thurman seemed delighted that I had got the picture, in however rudimentary a way. 'Absolutely!' he exploded. 'Although one thing you have to remember is that this is like the *sub*-subconscious. It is below even the subconscious.'

He went on to explain how it all worked. 'For example, a big act of generosity, a big sacrifice, or the overcoming of a rage where you forgive someone instead, those sort of big shifts of the mind register as a kind of DNA increment of generosity. On the other hand, if you become incredibly greedy or murdered someone that would make a big DNA increment of avarice or viciousness.

'These deeper, more powerful deeds or thoughts would register something that would really have an impact in another life. In fact everything registers somehow, but it's like a tiny little side-chain in the molecule combinations, if we're using the DNA analogy. It doesn't mean that every little impression makes a big change. But the indestructible drop is very sensitive and picks up everything. That's what guarantees, in the Buddhist world view, the idea that every little thing will build into something. A tiny bit of generosity will build into a good fruit, or a tiny bit of morality, or meditative insight. Whatever it is, will build.'

According to the Tibetan Buddhists it is this spiritual gene, with all its information encoded in it, which a person takes with them when they die. The time-honoured death process that is described so vividly in *The Tibetan Book of the Dead* explains exactly what happens. As we begin to withdraw from this life the elements of our physical form are one by one absorbed, and as that happens the consciousness becomes more and more fine, more and more subtle, more and more lucid as the gross conceptual mind retreats. Finally the most subtle consciousness that resides in the vicinity of our heart chankra is released and revealed. It is then, according to the Buddhist scriptures, that the most prominent, most powerful 'information' we hold comes to the fore and shapes our next existence.

Bob Thurman, who had just finished a new translation of *The Tibetan Book of the Dead*, described it in these words. 'The Bardo Being, the being who has died and is between lives, is in a state like a dream. By pure imagery it creates a sense of having a certain body. It's like when we dream now – we can become a butterfly or a horse, or we can change our gender. Different things happen to us in a dream. And we see them. But with what? We don't see with these eyes,' he said, indicating his own. 'So, your inner mental imagery produces a virtual eye. It's like a virtual reality awareness.'

Was this the reason, I asked, why Buddhists believe we can be reborn in many different forms, from very hell-like beings through to animals? 'Although I understand in principle that our mind creates our reality, I have never understood, nor accepted, that someone who has the mind of a human can possibly be reborn as an ant or a cockroach. What has happened to the rest of the awareness? Where has all the information of the human which has been encoded in the spiritual gene gone?' I asked.

Professor Thurman, as I expected, was ready with an answer. 'In order to descend that far back down the chain to a very simple kind of animal like a cockroach – although from a Buddhist point of view animals are not so far down as hell-beings, for example – would mean some enormous deed in a human life which has closed the sensibilities. It could be something which involved some incredible shock, terror or a huge recoiling. For example, a very vicious act that would make the person recoil from having been so brutal. It would take a very big negative action to permeate this DNA code so drastically as to make you select, imagery-wise, the form of a cockroach in your "between state". You see, the reason for being reborn as a cockroach is because from the "between state" you're attracted to the cockroach form. If you're reborn as a human you're attracted to the human form in that "between state". You gravitate to the life realms that you are predisposed to. To come to where you thought that little Joe cockroach was attractive you'd have to go through a huge shock.

'They say that when you're in the extremely subtle body/mind state of the between it's like being in a dream where your embodiment, because it is only created by imagery, is very unstable. So if you have these unconscious images that helplessly emerge where you might suddenly like the idea of being, say, a tarantula, you're in danger,' he said.

This was not comforting news. As I well knew from my own small excursions into meditation, the contents of one's mind are abysmally haphazard and generally out of control. The very act of sitting down and attempting to still the mind in the act of meditation reveals in dazzling Technicolor how irrelevant and futile most of the thoughts and images are that crowd into the mirror of your mind. This uncontrolled mind, according to Bob Thurman and all the sages, is what we are left with when the body packs up and all we are faced with are the impulses of our consciousness.

'Oh yes, Buddhists are afraid of the rebirth transition,' agreed Bob. 'They might not be afraid of eternal damnation, like Bible-thumping Christians, but they *are* afraid of rebirth. They don't think, "Oh, great, I'll be Cleopatra next time, so everything's fine." The transition is so vulnerable, you see, when you don't have control of your unconscious. That's why Buddhists spend so much energy in their life trying to influence this gene, trying to improve it. They call the lower realms the Abyss of the Three Wretched States or the Three Horrid States,' he added.

Over the years I had had a hard time accepting the actuality of hell. I recalled how Lama Zopa in those early Kopan days would spend days describing in graphic detail the various tortures, atrocities, pain and anguish of the 'lower realms'. They had a distinct Dante-esque flavour, with hapless creatures being impaled on spears, burning in fire, being constantly flayed or in a perpetual state of agonizing thirst and hunger. I rationalized them on the grounds that this was a medieval teaching still being taught in the feudal system that prevailed in Tibet when the Chinese came and the lamas fled.

Since Lama Zopa was clearly not given to lying, and since I could happily accept the happy things they told me about the absolute nature of reality and universal compassion, I attempted to translate the news of the hell realms into modern concepts that seemed acceptable. If all our existence is, as the Buddhists tell us, merely states of mind, why shouldn't these hell and animal realms be also, I reasoned. Would not a political prisoner being sadistically tortured, or a person caught up in the famine of Africa or the war zone of Bosnia, or a child suffering perpetual sexual abuse, be in a hell? The daily papers were full of news from all around the world of people undergoing terrible suffering. And what of those tormented souls with mental illness? Our society was full of them. Don't they also live in a kind of hell?

Just as I was settling down to my own interpretation of the Buddhist teachings of the six realms of existence, I was totally shaken by an interview I conducted with Dr Margot Grey, a psychologist and practising psychotherapist in a large and reputable London hospital whom I interviewed for a story

I was asked to do on Near Death Experiences. I discovered that while on holiday in India Margot Grey had had a NDE herself, which resulted in a personal and professional interest in the phenomenon. After lengthy research on the subject she wrote an excellent book called *Return from Death* (Arkana). Much to my interest, and alarm, Dr Grey told me of cases she had come across where people had described descending into horrific hell-like scenarios as they left their body and headed for the realm after death.

This was not only unnerving but unusual, as most descriptions of NDE are beatific and beautiful in the extreme. People tell of going towards the light, being embraced by love, feeling indescribably peaceful, being met by loved ones, and seeing exquisite places of unparalleled beauty. The negative experiences were hardly ever divulged, Dr Grey said, probably because people were too ashamed to tell about them. Nevertheless, they did exist.

She quoted cases where people had felt extreme 'fear and panic' and underwent 'mental and emotional anguish' as they sped 'downwards' towards a terrible place which was often described as 'barren', 'grey' or 'gloomy', which smelt of 'decay', and which was either extremely hot or piercingly cold. They told of travelling through 'black space' or 'a black vortex'. Sometimes they had visions of being threatened and taunted by wrathful demonic creatures; sometimes they were attacked by faceless, hooded figures. Sometimes there was a smell of sulphur and terrible cries and wailings.

While my blood was turning decidedly chilly at these accounts she told me of a specific case which illustrated her point. It centred on a woman whom she had treated in her capacity as a psychotherapist and who was still suffering from the after-effects of her terrifying NDE. As she was dying, this woman had found herself in a place surrounded by mist. It was, she said, extremely hot with a big pit belching forth vapour. There were arms and hands coming out of the pit trying to grab her. To her mind she was in hell. Then she saw an enormous lion bounding towards her from the other side and she screamed, petrified that it would push her into the pit. She remained in a state of semi-consciousness for about three days, and then revived.

The extraordinary aspect of this case history was that the woman was a devout, church-going Christian, who believed she had led a good moral life. She could not understand what she had done to deserve such a horrific punishment. Through her therapy the woman discovered that actually she was full of fury towards her husband, who had left her for a younger woman. According to Dr Grey, it was this rage held within her mind stream that had created the hell-like environment she had found herself in as her consciousness left her body. Together they worked to eradicate her anger and to become reconciled to what had happened.

This story fascinated me, because in spite of its entirely Western context it tallied exactly with what Lama Yeshe and particularly Lama Zopa had always maintained – that anger was one of the prime negative minds to be eliminated at all costs. It was one of our root delusions, along with greed and ignorance, and was guaranteed to cause us (and others) unmitigated suffering and pain. From the Buddhist point of view it was not God who condemned us to hell, but the state and content of our own minds. We create our reality, whatever it may be. It was a satisfactory explanation, if not a comforting one.

Later, watching an Oprah Winfrey show on NDE, I saw other people who claimed they had had a frightening or 'negative' experience. One young woman in particular described how, while she was 'unconscious' and apparently dying in a hospital bed, she saw ghouls close in around her ready to snatch her away. She was so convinced that what she had gone through was real that she had become a missionary to 'try to eradicate some of my selfishness', to use her words.

Thinking it all over, I came to the conclusion that all of this phantasmagorical scheme – the hell realms, animal realms, humans, gods, demi-gods, tulkus – in fact the whole issue of rebirth and reincarnation, hinged on just one crucial question. Does our consciousness, our mind, exist separately from our bodies, or not? If it does, as the Buddhists claim, then the possibility of our finding ourselves in other worlds after we die is great. It is also likely that we could have had numberless existences before we came into this present life. But if it didn't, the whole belief in rebirth and reincarnation simply collapsed. If consciousness was the same as our body, we would cease to exist at our death. It was as simple, and as complex, as that.

This was where the huge debate currently being waged in Western science came in. Was the mind the same as the brain? they were arguing. Where did consciousness come from? Although I had absolutely no expertise in the sphere of modern physics I was sufficiently fuelled by my interest in Buddhism to make at least a layperson's attempt to understand what the great minds (or should that be brains?) were saying. It was of the utmost importance. His Holiness the Dalai Lama thought so too. With his own predilection for science and his innate wisdom about the Buddhist explanation of things, he was regularly inviting scientists to debate the issue of mind in the spirit of genuine enquiry. Both sides, East and West, were, after all, seekers of truth. At a meeting which he convened in Dharamsala between himself, his most learned lamas and a group of cognitive scientists, the Dalai Lama succintly expressed the significance of the discussion.

'It is most important for the traditions of Western science and Eastern mental development to work together,' he said. 'At some stage people have gained the impression that these two traditions are very different and incompatible. In recent years, however, it has become clear that this is not the case. This kind of dialogue is therefore extremely important as a means of contributing something towards future humanity, by enabling each tradition to benefit from the other. So this is one goal.

'I also think it is important for Buddhists to understand the latest scientific findings concerning the nature of mind, the relationship between the mind and the brain, and the nature of consciousness – these sorts of things. Whether consciousness does or does not exist as a discrete entity, for example. I would like to introduce some of these Western explanations to Buddhists in general and to Tibetan Buddhists in particular.'

From my limited grasp of the debate I gathered that there was a large band of scientists now coming forward who called themselves 'scientific materialists' or 'reductionists'. They maintained that consciousness, our awareness, is merely a product of our nervous system, which in itself is composed of nothing but matter and energy. As such, our mind is the result of evolution starting from the Big Bang. Francis Crick, co-discoverer of DNA and author of *The Astonishing Hypothesis*, actually says that in his view conscious awareness in higher animals and humans has something to do with the rate at which brain cells oscillate or buzz. As such, the reductionists say that when the neurosystem ceases to function our consciousness vanishes. When we die, all that remains is a heap of rotting flesh. In other words, according to the reductionists we are reduced to nothing more than the sum of our molecules.

This theory has sparked off a veritable war among the egg-heads. Passions are running high. 'What accounts for the smell of the rose, the feeling of love, of pain, of the individual's unique view of the world?' ask the anti-materialists, and there are many of them. 'What, other than consciousness, has produced the materialistic view?' they ask.

While I was with Professor Thurman I took the opportunity to ask his view on the current mind/brain controversy. His eyes lit up.

'I love to debate this subject with materialists – it's one of my favourite things. I run into it all the time,' he said with relish. 'The idea of radical discontinuity or something becoming nothing is a category mistake. It's a Wittgensteinian failure and a completely silly idea! That is the ultimate wishful thinking. Just pull the trigger and all your problems are over – automatic Nirvana by messing up the brain,' he exploded.

'In nature we never observe something becoming nothing. Everything has an effect. Why should there suddenly be some notion of something becoming nothing? Basically it is incoherent. To say that sentient beings become nothing is a category mistake – because nothing is nothing. You can't therefore become it!' he roared. He paused, contemplating the implication that scientific materialism had on the notion of rebirth.

'Westerners think that it's some big, grown-up, mature thing to be a materialist, because they feel they are facing the fear of death – whereas Buddhists are somehow using wishful thinking by believing they go on and on in countless lives,' he continued. 'Ironically, what they don't understand is that the people who face a future life are scared about the quality of that future life much more than someone who faces obliteration. Obliteration is an anaesthetic. There's no pain in it. I would say that obliteration is an escape!

'Basically, the only way these scientists deal with the issue of rebirth is by being dismissive. They don't really examine any evidence. If they did, they wouldn't be able to dismiss it so readily,' he said.

Behind the controversy, the intellectual bickering and the high-minded concepts which appear to be so remote from the business of everyday life lies an issue of the utmost importance, one that promises to touch the ordinary man, woman and child in a profound and far-reaching way. Ultimately, what is at stake is the definition of human identity in the twenty-first century. Whether we decide we are nothing more than a lump of flesh or whether we find we do, indeed, have a soul will determine our behaviour, our moral codes, our education, the core of our belief systems and the very quality of life for many years to come.

Personally I admired the Dalai Lama's open-minded view when faced with the new science: 'Due to environmental factors one is subconsciously conditioned, and as a result may want to explain or discover something but be unable to do so successfully or completely. It is my view that in this respect the approaches of Buddhism in general and Mahayana Buddhism in particular are very much scientific approaches. Because some elements of the Buddha's teaching are incompatible with our knowledge of the world today, the final validation has to depend on the authority of reasoning and logic. Through investigation and analysis we arrive at fact, and even that fact appears to contradict the Buddha's own words – it doesn't matter.' Later he added, 'If there is good, strong evidence from science that such-and-such is the case, then we will change.' The Dalai Lama was demonstrating the first law of Buddhism: reality must be looked straight in the face if truth and freedom are to be found. It was a noble, honest stance. For all his words about logic and reasoning I have to admit, however, that when I look at the wise and humble monk called Tenzin Gyatso, the fourteenth Dalai Lama of Tibet, what touches me is not a mass of 'buzzing molecules' but the palpable, powerful compassion which emanates from him. In the end it seems that has very little to do with the brain and everything to do with the heart.

6

RABBI GERSHOM

My investigation to find the gurus of Western reincarnation brought me into contact with the most unlikely people. The most surprising, by far, was a Hasidic Jew living near Minneapolis, who had the most fantastic story to tell. Rabbi Yonassan Gershom had come into contact with hundreds of people who, he claimed, had died in the Holocaust and been born into the present time. Many of them, he said, were Gentiles.

News of this extraordinary evidence reached me soon after I arrived in New York, when someone showed me a copy of Rabbi Gershom's then new book *Beyond the Ashes – Cases of Reincarnation from the Holocaust* (ARE Press). I immediately decided to track the author down. What amazed me was not so much that Jewish people who had died in the Nazi concentration camps should be coming back to earth in new bodies (I was well enough acquainted with reincarnation to deem that possible), but that a rabbi, and a Hasidic rabbi to boot, should be documenting it and presenting his evidence to the world at large.

I had seen Hasidic Jews before, of course, especially in New York – the men with their long side ringlets, black hats and long beards, the women with wigs covering their ritually shaved heads – and had been rather nervous of them. They looked so austere – a somewhat closed and insular group, I felt. I had heard that they were ultra-orthodox, bent on bringing Jews back to Judaism, and that they followed Jewish law to the letter. These were certainly the last people I would have expected to embrace such a New Age idea as reincarnation. But my ignorance was well and truly blasted when I managed to track Rabbi Gershom down and speak to him.

'Hasidic Jews certainly believe in reincarnation,' he began. 'I myself have reason to believe I was a rabbi's son who was shot in a village in eastern Europe, and I know many members of the Hasidic community who are deliberately having large families in order to give bodies to the souls who died in the Holocaust,' he said.

He went on to tell me that Isaac Luria, a sixteenth-century rabbi and one of the greatest Jewish mystics of all time, taught reincarnation, as did Israel ben Aliezer, known as the Baal Shem Tov, who founded the Hasidic movement. 'Both these men were reputedly accurate past-life readers as well,' he explained. 'Their reincarnation stories abound, in both written and oral form – millions of Jews have heard of these teachings. In fact the Lubovitcher version of the Hasidic prayer book contains a bedtime prayer in which the supplicant forgives "anyone who has angered or vexed me . . . in this incarnation or any other".'

As the interview progressed I was to find out that Rabbi Gershom was a veritable fount of Jewish scholarship who spoke rapidly and eloquently on his subject. I was now learning that the Hasidic Jews, in spite of their rather fearsome appearance, considered themselves the mystics of the Jewish religion, the seers and visionaries. To them reincarnation was not just an idea, but a strongly held belief.

'The trouble is that there is a great deal of ignorance about what Jews really are. People in a Christian culture confuse the Old Testament studies, which are Christian, with Judaism, which is Jewish. You won't find the rich source of Jewish spirituality in the Old Testament,' he added.

Admonished, I learned more about Rabbi Gershom. He was a young man who had been ordained by Rabbi Zalman Schacter-Shalomi, the famous pioneer in Jewish spiritual renewal. He called himself a 'neo-Hasidic'. Not only was Rabbi Gershom an expert in Judaism, but he had also delved deeply into other faiths and into the movements of the New Age, including metaphysics. I discovered that he ran workshops on reincarnation, mingled with native American Indians, taught at the Institute of Adult Jewish Studies in Minneapolis and served as a chaplain in a nursing home. Not least, he has lent his ear to countless worried people in the role of counsellor.

It was in this last capacity that he heard of the reincarnation of the Holocaust victims. The first incident took him completely by surprise. The year was 1981 and Rabbi Gershom was sitting by himself at home – he had cancelled his discussion group on the kabbalah and esoteric Jewish teachings due to the heavy snowfall. But a young blonde Norwegian woman knocked on his door anyway. After he had given her a cup of coffee, she announced that what she really wanted to talk about was the Holocaust.

She told Rabbi Gershom that ever since childhood the very mention of the Holocaust had filled her with an unaccountable fear. Recently her sister had been sharing with her some material she was studying on the concentration camps, and this was adding to her terror. As the young woman was talking Rabbi Gershom 'saw' another face, thin and emaciated, superimposed on the beautiful young face before him; spurred on by some intuition, he began to hum a tune. Then the girl's eyes grew wide with dread and she broke down in sobs, saying that she knew she had died in the Holocaust. The song that Rabbi Gershom had sung was 'Ani Maamin', the hymn sung by many thousands of Jews as they entered the gas chambers. Until that moment the Norwegian woman had never heard the song – in this life, at least.

This was to be the first of an amazing number of Holocaust reincarnation stories that were to come Rabbi Gershom's way as word spread that he was receptive to hearing such reports. For several years he kept quiet about the 'hot' property that he was holding, fearing that if the media got hold of this sensitive material it would be horribly sensationalized (which eventually it was). He also felt that the public was not ready to face a literal revival of the crimes of the concentration camps. He knew he was right when the Spiritual Frontiers Fellowship in America turned down a talk about his 'discovery' on the grounds that the Holocaust reincarnations were too heavy and upsetting. Guilt and fear were obviously at play.

Now, he deems, the time is ripe. Rabbi Gershom can tell his stories of the many people he has met who he is convinced died at the hands of the Nazis in the Holocaust, only to be reborn in our present time. Although he believes there are many such people born again as Jews, he has concentrated on the accounts of those born into Gentile families because, he says reasonably, the proof of reincarnation is more convincing in these cases. Small children who have not been surrounded by the customs, thoughts and faith of the Jewish religion, and yet who show an uncanny knowledge of these things, are definitely to be taken seriously. Their childhood memories, if not dependent on nurture and environment, need some explanation.

To illustrate his point he tells of the Lutheran housewife who every Friday night had a strong urge to light candles. This compulsion had no basis in her own faith nor did it have any meaning for her family. Rabbi Gershom told her that for thousands of years Jewish women the world over had kindled the Sabbath lights on Friday, and had even tried to continue this custom in the crowded railway wagons on the way to the concentration camps. And then there was the man, non-Jewish, who related that his toddler son would refuse to drink milk if there was meat on the table. If his parents insisted, the child would throw the milk on to the floor. They were perplexed at this behaviour, since their son never acted like this if the drink was juice or water. It is not Kosher for a Jew to eat meat and milk at the same meal, and Rabbi Gershom suggested that the child's behaviour was possibly a carry-over from a past life.

He tells of the recurring nightmares that many of the people he met had experienced as children. These nightmares are, he says, so authentic in their detail that they constitute proof that these people had actually lived before and experienced the events of which they now dreamed.

There was Beverly, a single mother in her thirties, who dreamed she was a little boy of about seven or eight, standing in a line with his mother. Beverly described how they got to a table where a man was telling some people to go to the left and others to the right. He pointed and they went through a door. Then the scene would shift and the boy and his mother would be in a place where there was a terrible smell. In her nightmare she saw men throwing people into a fire alive, and then the little boy was thrown in too. He would pat himself, trying to put out the flames; then he died.

There were those who had memories of being buried alive, of seeing men with guns and black boots towering over them while more and more dirt was thrown on their faces as they lay buried in a pit; those who saw blood on the snow; those who had an inexplicable fear of barbed wire; others who were terrified of uniforms, police, sirens. By the time he wrote his book Rabbi Gershom had collected some two hundred and fifty accounts of Holocaust reincarnations, and since then the number has grown considerably.

'I would say there are thousands of cases. Since the book was published I've had at least a hundred letters from all over the world – from people in Chile, Australia, France, Germany, Canada. I've talked personally to about five hundred people. At every conference I go to another four or five people come up to me and tell me they believe they are Holocaust reincarnations. Actually I've stopped counting. This is just the tip of the iceberg, I would say,' he told me.

This was impressive, and the evidence that Rabbi Gershom gave was convincing. But, he said, he had more in mind when he wrote the book than telling stories of past lives – there was much more behind the discovery of reincarnated Holocaust victims than that. 'I wanted to give a theological interpretation of what the Holocaust was all about,' he stated. 'There are an awful lot of people for whom the Holocaust is a karmic payback for something. They do not see Judaism as a religion worth dying for. So they can't see the Holocaust as being martyrdom for a higher purpose.'

I had heard these theories expounded several times by Western experts in reincarnation, who believed that the millions of Jewish deaths in the concentration camps were 'group karma' being paid off from previous negative group actions committed in the past. Events in history like the Spanish Inquisition or the atrocities committed by the marauding Mongol hordes were often quoted.

Rabbi Gershom was having none of it. 'A lot of people say we had it coming to us – that the Holocaust was a punishment for being rip-off money-lenders, or other crimes. It's very anti-Semitic. I did not find a single case, from the people I met who remembered their past lives, where somebody tortured another human being in the Spanish Inquisition and therefore was tortured in the Holocaust,' he said somewhat heatedly.

I admitted I was confused. The laws of karma, as I had been taught them by the Buddhists, were unchangeable. We ourselves carried the cause for our situation on our mind stream, and no one else was involved. One couldn't shift the responsibility, but that didn't mean there was any blame. The lamas had said that we had all committed umpteen negative deeds in the past, which would ripen as future suffering. After all, every one of us suffered from delusions. Personally I had always been rather impressed that my teachers hadn't shifted the goalposts when it came to themselves. I had heard Lama Zopa say, more than once, that the TB he had suffered from when he was young was definitely the result of negative karma in the past. Even the Dalai Lama, who every week listens to the outpourings of anguish from his countrymen and women about the atrocities in Tibet, has publicly said that the present sufferings of his people were indubitably caused by collective wrong-doings in the past. (Although, he added, this did not mean that one should sit idly by and let the Chinese persecutions continue.)

'Do you not believe in karma?' I asked Rabbi Gershom.

'Yes, but not defined in quite the same way. The thing is, it's not tit-for-tat. As I said, out of all the people who remembered their past lives I did not find a single one who had tortured someone in the Inquisition and was tortured themselves in the Holocaust. I did, however, find many people who had died as a martyr in the Inquisition who also died as a martyr in the Holocaust,' he said. It seemed like a completely new slant on the matter.

According to Rabbi Gershom, the reasons behind the imprisonment and persecution of the Jews in World War II went far deeper than karma. They were both mystical and highly esoteric, and were eventually the explanation as to why Jews had been persecuted through the ages.

'The Covenant of Sinai, where the Ten Commandments were given, was much more than most people realize. It was a cosmic event that transcends all incarnations and which binds Jews together for all their incarnations to be witness to the Oneness of God. When there are dictators they tend to go after the Jews first because we do not bow to anyone but God. We are witnesses to certain principles, and so are the first to be attacked when those principles are in danger.'

This was a little vague. I pressed him to tell me what those principles were that caused dictators such as Hitler to persecute the Jews. His answer took me into the heart of Jewish mysticism and was breathtaking both in its vastness and in its implications.

'We are keeping time and space in balance,' he said. 'That is why the Jews are said to be "chosen". We are chosen not in the sense that we are special, or the favourite, or better than anyone else, but because we have been selected for a certain task. If the planet is one society, the priesthood for certain tasks is the Jewish people. From a kabbalistic, mystical point of view that is what we are doing. However,' he added hastily, 'you won't find your average reform Rabbi telling you this!'

He elaborated on how keeping time and space in balance worked. 'For example, from a Hasidic standpoint the Sabbath really is a different time. The time is created and flows through the prayers of the Jewish people. Similarly the 613 commandments or Mitzvahs – known as the Mitvot – were given collectively to the Jewish people to perform. Now those 613 Mitvahs correspond to spiritual energies, so when a Jew is doing one of them it is not only the physical meaning that matters, it also has an effect on the cosmic vibration of the universe.'

It was based, he said, on the mystical meaning of the Hebrew alphabet. The three 'mother letters' represent the elements of air, water and fire out of which God created earth. The seven double letters represent days of the week and the duality of positive and negative, good and evil and so forth. The twelve single letters correspond to the twelve months of the year. All these components also corresponded to body parts and to time and space.

'So we're bringing together thought, speech, physical action and time. That's the primal vibration of the universe,' he told me. 'Interestingly, at a recent seminar I heard that one of the space missions which was measuring the vibrational levels of various planets discovered that the hertz level at which the earth vibrates is the same as the human voice.

'There has always been a legend that if one were pure and holy enough, and understood the combinations of the Hebrew letters (which are the building-blocks of the universe), one could create life. That's where the stories of the Golem of Prague and Frankenstein's monster came from. The Golem of Prague was created to protect the Jews from Christian persecution. In reality, when humans are imperfect and try to create life you end up with imperfect creations, which get out of control and have to be destroyed.

'Anyway, the kabbalistic system based in Isaac Luria has this belief about Tikkun Olam, which means literally: Repair the World. It could roughly be translated as "planetary healing". The idea is that when Jews are doing the commandments, with spoken intention, the vibrational quality of those acts affects the universe and repairs and elevates the vibration of the planet.'

Back to Hitler and his part in this mystical drama: according to Rabbi Gershom, it was this supreme task given to the Jews that Hitler was out to destroy. 'Many people believe that Hitler was into black magic – that he was channelling very negative energies. Obviously anyone who wanted to rule the world would go after the Jews, who are repairing the vibrational quality of the planet. I personally believe that this was the battle of the Sons of the Light versus the Sons of Darkness foretold in the Essene writings,' he said.

This statement could have appeared utterly bizarre and unbelievable had I not heard before of Hitler's dabbling in black magic and the occult. The Führer's involvement with the Thule Society, one of the most influential occult groups in Germany, was well known, as was his taking of the consciousness-altering drug peyote and his fascination with mysticism. Alfred Rosenberg, Hitler's official theologian, whose book *Myth of the Twentieth Century* advocated that Western civilization should be purged of all things Jewish, was also a member of the Thule Society. Perhaps what Rabbi Gershom was saying was not so outlandish. What he was telling me, in short, was that the group karma that the Holocaust victims had experienced was not so much the result of negative harmful deeds committed collectively in the past, as a sacrifice made *en masse* for a higher purpose.

It was a completely different perspective from the Eastern view, and one which I found fascinating if not entirely logical. Surely there still had to be *cause* for any phenomenon, and personal responsibility taken for it. I wondered how the scholarly Rabbi Gershom would go in a round of debate with the equally scholarly Lamas. It was a sight I would have loved to have witnessed.

Rabbi Gershom also had other new views of reincarnation which I had to take on board. I asked him if Judaism believed that people could move both upwards and downwards in the reincarnation game, as the Eastern pundits claimed.

'Oh yes, people can slide backwards,' he replied. 'We believe that denying Judaism is a step backwards,' This was another startling dissimilarity, for never had I heard it said that to change faiths was a black mark on the karmic roll book.

'In our teachings it is said that the core group at the Covenant of Sinai always come back as Jews, and that it is a step backwards on the spiritual ladder to be born as a non-Jew. Of course there are some individuals who wander in and out of Judaism but there are those souls who are like lighthouses, that are always there specializing and learning one path very deeply for many incarnations. Personally I believe that the trauma of the Holocaust has driven many Jews from their own religion to seek other spiritual paths. They died thinking "If I am being starved and tortured and persecuted because of my religion, then I do not want to be a Jew any more." In their suffering and haste to come back they grabbed the first body they could get. But their souls are still Jewish. Many of the reincarnated Holocaust victims who came back as Gentiles either have converted to Judaism or are thinking of doing so.

'You see, the Holocaust was more than just killing of people, which was bad enough – it was also an attempt to destroy the spiritual power of Judaism. Very sadly, it halfway succeeded. In America especially there is so little spirituality among Jews – they are very anti-orthodox. I feel there is a lot of fear involved in being an observant Jew,' he said.

'One woman who was converting back to Judaism said she felt the reason why so many people came back as non-Jews was because the Holocaust had so totally crushed the spirit of the Jewish people. Any child growing up as a Jew in the fifties would have had this horrible pall of death, destruction, depression and grief, and so they chose to come back in non-Jewish bodies where they could experience a secure, joyful childhood and then convert back to Judaism to bring the joy back.

'Personally, I believe that all of those souls who are part of the Covenant of Sinai will return to being Jews. It is their karmic roots,' he said.

I couldn't resist asking him if he thought the Nazis were reincarnating too.

'Yes, I certainly believe that the Nazis are returning. It would be ridiculous to think that only innocent souls reincarnate! I have not had any opportunity personally to meet reincarnated individuals who still believe in Nazism, but if we consider the recent resurgence of right-wing organizations in America and around the world, then it is not too difficult to believe that the souls who were Nazis in a previous life are once again among us. Some, no doubt, would have learnt from their mistakes and progressed beyond fascism. But I believe there are many other souls who are repeating the same mistakes this time around,' he said.

Although as a rabbi he is not personally sought out by many former Nazis, he spoke of one Christian mother who came to him concerned about her teenage daughter's sudden obsession with Nazi paraphernalia, which certainly did not stem from the tolerant, peace-loving home in which she was brought up. The girl also loved motorcycles, fast cars – anything with a roaring engine, in fact. She was not anti-Semitic, however. Rabbi Gershom concluded that this could well be a past-life carry-over from a young man, possibly a pilot, who had been captivated by the excitement of the outer trappings of the Nazi military might.

Among the many things I learned about reincarnation from the mystical Jewish perspective was their explanation of what it is that goes from one existence to another, experiencing different lives. It was just as complex and profound as the Tibetan Buddhists', but again radically different in concept and meaning.

According to Rabbi Gershom the thing that travels from one incarnation to the next is a 'soul', although according to its Hebrew definitions the 'soul' has many different meanings and interpretations. The rabbi believes there are five levels to the soul, which, in the light of modern psychology and metaphysics, he defines as:

1 *nefresh*, the biological life force of the body
2 *ruach*, the lower emotional spirit or 'ego'
3 *neshamah*, the individual higher consciousness
4 *chayah*, the collective unconscious of the group
5 *yechida*, the level of unity with creation and God.

Rabbi Gershom holds that the first two levels do not survive beyond death because they are dependent on the physical body. *Neshamah*, however, does survive and can be consciously developed. It is at this level that all the soul's incarnations are remembered between earth lives – not every detail, but the lessons and truths significant to the spiritual growth of the individual soul. In addition, the *neshamah* maintains a constant connection to the *chayah* and *yechidah*, the higher transcendental levels where the soul touches the light of the All-Knowing God.

Rabbi Gershom likens *chayah* to Jung's collective unconscious, where you are linked to your particular karmic group. As for the highest level, *yechidah*, here the soul is united with all creation and touches its origin in the mind of the Creator. Judaism does not believe that one can actually become God (whereas Buddhists believe everyone can become a Buddha), but one can get plugged into the source of Divine Light and Creation in the same way that a light bulb gets plugged into the electricity being put out by the power station.

These were highly sophisticated, intellectually challenging arguments. I felt I would have to return to them later, when I had more time, in order to examine the profundity of the Jewish notion of what a soul is. For all the differences, however, I was already discovering many similarities between the Eastern and Jewish views on past, present and future lives.

I heard that, like the Buddhists, Jews understand that we return many, many times, as both male and female, and that the precise circumstances of each incarnation are never the same. Similarly, negative karma or 'sins' are projected forward into future lives until the karma has been paid for. I heard that

Hasidic Jews, like the Buddhists, believe that each life presents a precious opportunity for spiritual growth and that this is the essence of being human. The problems we have, the troubles we run into, should therefore be viewed as opportunities for advancement, not as a means for self-pity. The most heartening meeting-point between East and West was that both shared a remarkably similar end goal.

'What is the final destination of reincarnation in the Jewish tradition?' I asked Rabbi Gershom.

'The goal is to remain in the spiritual world – to return to the Garden of Eden, that is our metaphor. Once a soul has reached that exalted pinnacle it no longer needs to return to this earth to learn its karmic lessons. Judaism preaches that these elevated beings return voluntarily, sometimes for thousands of incarnations, in order to help the rest of humankind. They are called the Zaddikim or 'righteous holy ones'. While some Zaddikim are openly recognized, some come to this earth as ordinary human beings and do their work in disguise, as it were. It is said that there are always at least thirty-six hidden Jewish saints on this earth, leading exemplary lives and helping the world turn on its axis.'

Were these the Jewish versions of the bodhisattvas – the beings who renounced their place in Nirvana in order to return to help other living beings? As if to confirm my hypothesis the rabbi added: 'In the Eastern traditions you have gurus who come back as gurus. The Jewish tradition has its Enlightened Masters too, ones who are beyond the law of cause and effect. These are the ones who come to preserve and pass on our wisdom.'

I came away from the interview fascinated by what I had learnt about the Hasidic Jewish religion and Rabbi Gershom's challenging views on reincarnation. I could not accept all that he had said, but I heartily agreed with him that, if the world would stop persecuting the Jews and allow them to fulfil the beauty and profundity of their spiritual task, and to disperse their spiritual teachings, the world would be much richer for it.

7

THE FRENCH CONNECTION

The next stop in my search to discover the new Western tulkus was France. All tulkus, by definition, are exceedingly interesting, and the one I was to meet here was no exception. The small boy I was about to be introduced to was, I had been told, the first recognized example of a Western-to-Western reincarnation. This was rare indeed, for until now I had only heard of, and met, Eastern masters who had been able to choose their rebirth at will. As I already knew, the reincarnation process was exceedingly difficult, requiring not only a refined understanding and mastery of the mind as it becomes increasingly subtle on leaving the gross physical body, but also a determination to return to this world to help sentient beings. If a Westerner had managed such an extraordinary feat it would be a milestone in occidental spiritual history.

What made this particular journey all the more interesting was that the subject in question was none other than Zina Rachevsky, the woman who had been Lama Yeshe's and Lama Zopa Rinpoche's first Western disciple. The story of Zina is as fascinating as that of her mentors, and is told in full in *The Boy Lama*. Anyone who had been to Kopan knew of her, and her life story had dazzled us all. She was by all accounts larger than life – a beautiful, wilful, unconventional woman who in keeping with her fairy-tale life was in fact an aristocrat of Russian descent, whom people called Princess. She had been brought up in California and became a sixties' Hollywood starlet. As such she experienced all the riches, glamour, attention and superficiality that Tinseltown had to offer, and all its pitfalls. She was said to be insecure and attention-seeking. There were drug scandals, lovers, several husbands, a determination to live life on the edge, and a deep spiritual dissatisfaction. She was, in many ways, just another child of her times.

So it was not surprising that, like thousands of other flower-power Californians, Zina made the trip to India in search of a guru. One day in 1965 she burst into the small room that Lama Yeshe and Lama Zopa shared in Darjeeling, enquiring of the startled inhabitants: 'How can I receive peace and liberation?'

The two lamas might well have been amazed, because up until that moment no Westerner had ever been to see them, let alone ask for the means to reach Enlightenment. They tentatively agreed to give Zina teaching, and after several months of daily visits her sincerity became obvious to both of them. In an interview I conducted with Lama Yeshe in London he told me how Zina had first appeared to him.

'She was very dissatisfied with everything. She said her life was empty, that it had no "taste". She had done everything in life, but still could find no satisfaction. I could understand what she was saying. In comparison I had nothing – no country, no home, no money, no possessions, no family, and yet I had everything. With Zina, and later with other Westerners, I began to enquire about their lifestyle. I realized that what Zina lacked was an understanding of herself, her inner life. She lacked an understanding of her own potential to be happy. She thought happiness came from without, but it does not. It comes from within,' he said.

Zina later became a Buddhist nun, the first Westerner to do so, and then went with Lama Yeshe and Lama Zopa to Nepal, an environment which her gurus thought conducive to her spiritual practice. There, near the great stupa of Boudnath, considered to be the most powerful Buddhist shrine outside Tibet, they set up small teaching courses for curious Westerners who came to see what this strange triumvirate were up to. The courses grew, and a centre was established on the hill called Kopan, overlooking Boudnath and the Kathmandu valley, with the mighty Himalayas as a backdrop. Inadvertently, the wild but searching Zina had begun a movement which was to grow into a worldwide organization and affect the lives of thousands.

Like all fairy stories, this one had an equally dramatic ending. On the advice of Lama Yeshe Zina left Kopan to embark on a long retreat high in the Himalayas. Just like the earlier yogis she settled in a cave, isolating herself from the distractions of life in Kathmandu, in order to enter profound meditation based on the tantric deity Yamantaka – a fierce-looking character, blue in colour, surrounded by flames, brandishing a sword and symbolizing the wrathful aspect of all the Buddhas' wisdom. For the previously fun-loving, gregarious Hollywood starlet used to all the trappings of a wealthy Western existence, this must have been an incredibly hard assignment. Up in the mountains conditions are tough. The weather is harsh, the terrain steep and treacherous, the food sparse and the physical comforts nil. But the air is clear and clean, the mountains hum with the collected power of generations of meditators, and those breathtaking vistas from the rooftop of the world are unparalleled for expanding the mind. Zina went – dutifully following her beloved Lama Yeshe's directive.

She had been in her cave for over a year when suddenly, at the age of forty-two, she died. Two rinpoches who were living in the area reported that while in meditation they had 'witnessed' Zina's passing, and were able to indicate the exact time and day of her death. No one quite knew why she had died – some said she had eaten poisoned food, others that she had contracted cholera. Whatever the reason, the illness was apparently sudden and lasted five days. On the morning of the fifth day she is said to have sat up and announced, 'I am going to die', and in her dying state managed to bring herself to the full lotus position and concentrate her mind on the spiritual practice which she had been developing in her retreat. Those

Tenzin Sherab, born Elijah Ary, at home in Montreal, Canada. As a small child he remembered his past life as a Tibetan meditational master and scholar.

Trinley Tulku, preparing once more to become a spiritual teacher, in his monastery in France.

A young Tenzin Sherab, in robes and already recognized as the reincarnation of the late Geshe Jatse, with Lama Yeshe in California.

Tenzin Sherab, installed in Sera, the great Tibetan monastery in southern India, heavily engaged in debate.

Jetsunma Ahkon Norbu Lhamo, born in Brooklyn, the first Western woman to be recognized as a reincarnation of a Tibetan spiritual adept.

Jetsunma Ahkon Norbu Lhamo, with the reincarnation of her brother from her former life. In the sixteenth century they founded a Tibetan lineage which continues to this day.

The Stupa Park, representing the Enlightened deeds of the Buddha, which Jetsunma has created and opened to the general public.

Jetsunma's Centre 'Kunzang Odsal Palyul Changchub Choling' or 'The Fully Awakened Dharma Place of Primordial Clear Light', at Poolesville, near Washington. It is now the Western seat of an unbroken Tibetan spiritual lineage.

The twenty-four-hour prayer vigil dedicated to ending the suffering of all sentient beings has been part of Jetsunma's mission even before she was recognized. It continues to this day.

Jetsunma's temple – an evocative mix of lit crystals and rows of thousands of Buddhas, an innovative blend of Western and traditional Tibetan styles.

Lama Osel (the Spanish-born reincarnation of Lama Thubten Yeshe) in Switzerland playing with the reincarnation of Geshe Rabtan, a major teacher of Tibetan Buddhism in the West.

Lama Osel with his classmates at Sera monastery, where he is receiving the traditional Tibetan Buddhist education.

A sole white face among the highest reincarnated Lamas of Tibetan Buddhism. *Left to right*: Lama Osel, Serkong Rinpoche, Ling Rinpoche, Trijang Rinpoche, Serkong Dorje Chang, Song Rinpoche.

His Holiness Dalai Lama cuts Lama Osel's hair, symbolizing his acceptance into the monastery.

Lama Osel with Ling Rinpoche, the reincarnation of the Dalai Lama's senior tutor.

Lama Osel having fun with a former Western attendant monk Namgyal.

Lama Osel in the traditional dress for Lama Dancing.

1994, Lama Osel with Lama Zopa Rinpoche and his new 'attendant', his father Paco.

Lama Osel in the traditional dress for Lama Dancing.

Lama Thubten Yeshe, the founder of a world-wide organization of Tibetan Buddhist centres, who died in California in March 1984, and was reincarnated as Lama Osel in Spain in February 1985.

who could see such things said that Zina was now in a pure land.

It seemed that with her death she had gone out of our lives. No one talked about the woman who had ignited the first flame of the movement that has been steadily growing ever since. That is, not until word got out that Zina's reincarnation had been found in France. The child was a boy, and his father was actually a relation of Zina's.

So it was with considerable curiosity that I made my way to France to see this child, now four years old, and to meet his parents. They had agreed to tell me their story on condition that I did not use the boy's name. The reason, they explained, was that His Holiness Sakya Trinzin, head of the Sakya sect of Tibetan Buddhism who had officially recognized the boy, had advised them to conceal their son's identity in order to protect him until he was old enough for his development to be secure. Fame, I realized, could well be a trap on the spiritual path; 'Also we do not want people projecting their imaginings and fantasies about Zina on to him,' his parents added. It seemed a reasonable request, and I agreed.

We met in an apartment in a smart Paris suburb, and over several hours discussed the phenomenon of reincarnation as they were experiencing it first hand. All the while Pierre, as I shall call the boy, demonstrated that remarkable level of energy and determination coupled with inherent sweetness that I had seen in the young Lama Osel. He was a lithe, attractive child with fine features, a mop of thick, fair hair and bright, lively, brown eyes. His face was animated, full of life and curiosity. He showed me his cars and trucks, telling me their names in French. He understands English, but refuses to speak it. Already at this age Pierre, it seems, is determined to carve out his separate and unique identity.

'He is very strong-willed, just like Zina,' said his mother Janine, a professional woman who runs her own business. As relatives of Zina they had heard tales of her exploits long before their son arrived on the scene. She and Pierre's father, Gérard, are now divorced but meet regularly to discuss their unusual child's upbringing. I had heard that Lama Osel's parents had also separated, and wondered if the strain of having a recognized reincarnation as a child was too much for a marriage to bear. In Tibet they say that when a tulku is born one of the parents often dies shortly afterwards. Who knows why? Perhaps there is a price to pay for having a 'special child' born into the world.

I asked Janine and Gérard if they believed their son was really a reincarnation of Zina, as they had been told.

'There has been a reincarnation, of that we are certain. But Pierre is not Zina. He is not a clone. He is his own person. Zina is not walking around in Pierre's body. Zina is Zina and Pierre is Pierre,' they said emphatically. And yet again I was reminded of the time when I asked Lama Osel outright if he were Lama Yeshe. He insisted: 'I am Lama Osel. Before I am Lama Yeshe, now Tenzin Osel, a monk.' The distinction, it seems, is subtle but of vital importance. The Buddha said that consciousness, like everything else in the universe, is in a state of constant flux. It is a stream of moments of awareness perpetually in motion. So I reasoned that there could be no fixed, concrete Zina or Lama Yeshe who had reappeared as someone else, any more than a rose that dies can be the same flower that you see blooming on the same bush. All one can accurately say, I thought, is that the stream of consciousness that was once labelled 'Zina' is said to be manifesting in a form which is now labelled 'Pierre'. It is as magnificent and as mysterious as that.

As I talked to Janine and Gérard, at least one concrete fact emerged very clearly. In spite of Zina's highly exotic, colourful and controversial past, they both held her in the highest regard. Neither has any doubt that she attained an extremely high level of spiritual accomplishment in her cave among those remote and awesome peaks during the last months of her life. Since Pierre was born they had come into contact with a journalist who had interviewed Zina while she was in retreat. The tapes which suddenly fell into their laps were like a gift from the pure realms. Hearing her voice and the words she spoke convinced them that here was a very special woman indeed.

'When I heard her voice I got goose pimples – she sounded like an angel,' commented Janine. 'Whatever she had done in the past, she had managed to turn her life around completely, of that I am sure. She said at one point, talking about her temptation to leave the lamas and go back to having a "good time", that she had decided against it because she knew from bitter experience that "the highs were so high, and the lows were so low". Those were her words exactly. I also remember her saying very clearly that people should not despise or think badly of those who take drugs, because in reality they are searching – searching for a spiritual life, something with meaning. Her words moved me deeply,' she said.

Later Gérard played me the tape and, although the interview was in French, I could hear that Zina's voice was surprisingly light and lyrical with an unmistakable ring of joy about it. Something profound and wonderful must have been happening to her in her mountain retreat.

Most significantly, the tape revealed words which offered conclusive proof that Zina intended to be reborn in exactly the same way as the Eastern tulkus. Gérard revealed the content of the tape.

Zina had told the reporter that she now had a clear understanding of the Bardo, the Tibetan term for the intermediate state between death and rebirth, and furthermore, that she had the *intention* to reincarnate. She was adamant. Her great wish was to prove to Westerners that they too could direct the course of their next rebirth. This desire, more than any material or worldly dream, was now her driving force. She insisted that what she spoke was the truth. Interestingly, her words were spoken some seventeen years before Pierre's appearance on this earth.

The interview with the French journalist who trekked up the mountain to see her also revealed the extent of the spiritual progress she had made. It was impressive and, for Westerners with aspirations, highly encouraging. If Zina could do it, so could we.

'Zina said that when she first started to meditate she couldn't stay for more than five minutes, but she resolutely made the effort to stay for longer and longer periods of time,' Gérard continued. She claimed that she could now stay for a few hours, and said that if, in a few months, she had managed to go from five minutes to a few hours, perhaps in a few years' time she would be able to stay in meditation for years. Eventually, like Lama Zopa in his previous life, she might be able to stay in a cave for twenty years.

Later a letter that Zina had written to Lama Yeshe came into my hands. More than anything it reflects the remarkable transformation, the profound understanding and exquisite state of mind that Zina had achieved before she died. It was yet more 'proof' of her spiritual mastery.

In it she revealed how her thoughts were already turned towards the suffering of sentient beings, and how miraculously the clarity of the vista on her high mountain peak was beginning to be mirrored in her mind.

More significantly, Zina spoke with some surprise of the improvement in her meditation since arriving at her 'cave'. She could, she claimed, now sit in stillness for some hours at a time, and with her mounting discipline, the goal which she was heading towards grew increasingly into focus. The sight of it filled her with awe. It was, she said, the achievement of Enlightenment and the mastery over death, no less.

The letter went on to say that although she had seen her final destination, she recognized in all humility that she still had a long way to go but now the path was marked and she knew her place on it. She spoke of her deepening awareness of her own shortcomings . . . those habitual tendencies of mind which she knew she had to overcome if she were to succeed.

Specifically she mentioned her foibles of irritation and its stronger aspect, anger . . . that great enemy of inner and outer peace. But she knew, she said, that the antidote was compassion, and increasingly she prayed for both patience and tolerance.

To my eyes the letter reverberated with honesty and an almost childlike simplicity, but above all it was the unmistakable great love she bore towards her lama that made the document so moving and utterly compelling.

She had signed it with her Tibetan name.

If Zina had died in the beatific state of mind that her letter conveys, she could indeed have conquered the rapids of the Bardo, the state between death and rebirth, to reach her goal – attaining the exact reincarnation she wanted, so as to prove that a Westerner could master what the great meditators of Tibet had done.

In the time before Pierre's birth, Zina's presence and personality began to make themselves felt with increasing intensity. It is a gripping tale which still fascinates Janine and Gérard. Gérard began to unravel for me the curious sequence of events by which Zina suddenly began to impinge herself upon their lives.

'It all began when I went back to Nice some months before I married Janine. I was reminded again of my cousin Zina (actually she was my grandmother's cousin) because the house where I was living was just five minutes' walk from the house where Zina's Russian family lived. Zina herself lived there for quite a long time and became Miss Côte D'Azur, or something like that. I remembered reading about it in the papers. After I returned to Nice, the Dalai Lama came to the South of France and the front page of the local paper, the *Nice Matin*, was full of pictures of him. So my mind was suddenly full of my cousin who had become a Tibetan nun,' he recalled.

'Even though I was young, I remember her very well. Whenever I saw her she was always semi-naked, walking around the house with very few clothes on. She had lots of husbands and children. She sent a lot of letters to my grandmother when she was in retreat. My grandmother used to show them to me. They were sort of crazy letters with a lot of drawings and poetry. I remember very clearly one day, when my grandmother had received another letter, her turning to my mother and saying, 'I'm sure she is using more and more drugs.' Which was totally untrue, of course.

'Anyhow, seeing Zina's house again and the Dalai Lama's visit recalled my cousin who had died in the Himalayan mountains back in 1973.'

The next development in this strange story happened after Gérard had decided to return to Paris – much against his family's and his friends' advice. He was studying law and felt somehow drawn back to the capital. One day he was in a shop buying a book on taxation. The queue at the counter was long and, as Gérard waited in line, a bright orange book with black lettering seemed to leap out at him from the shelf next to him. He took it down and flicked through the pages.

'I saw, in half a second, the name Zina Rachevsky. I went through the book more slowly but couldn't find the name again. As the queue was very long and slow I kept looking, and eventually found it among the first pages. The book was the French edition of *Wisdom Energy*, the first book on the teachings of Lama Yeshe and Lama Zopa Rinpoche. Zina was mentioned in the introduction, about how she was the first Western disciple of the two lamas. For me finding her name there was incredible.' He bought the book.

'Now I see why it was very important for me to leave Nice. All my friends said, "How can you do that?" I was deeply into the Japanese martial art of Aikido, attracted by the philosophy I found in it. But deep inside me I felt I had to go back to Paris. It was extremely important, but at the time I couldn't tell you why,' he added.

He read the book overnight, finding in it answers to questions he had long been asking. In particular he was drawn by the two lamas' discourses on karma – the law of cause and effect which states that nothing happens by accident or chance. Excited by his discovery he phoned his grandmother in Nice, who was writing a book about the

Russian side of the family, to tell her that he had information about her cousin. Instead of the usual disparagement about the exotic Zina, the response was positive. He then sat down to write to the editor of *Wisdom Energy*, to try to obtain more information on Zina, but never sent the letter.

A few months later, after he was married to Janine, he took the book down again to discuss its contents with a friend. They talked way into the night, thrashing out the concepts of Tibetan Buddhism in much the same way as Zina must have done when she first came into contact with this intellectually gritty religion.

The very next day Gérard had to attend a hearing in the Palais de Justice, but when he arrived he found it had been cancelled. With nothing to do, he went to browse in a big department store called La Samaritaine. Ironically, in the light of what was to follow, the store's advertising slogan was: One Finds All in La Samaritaine! As he was leaving and getting into the lift he caught, in a fraction of a second, a glimpse of maroon and gold, the specific colours of the robes of a Tibetan Buddhist monk. Compelled by something he was not sure of, he immediately took the lift back up again to find the person wearing those robes. He felt it was a sign. He searched for a while and eventually found the monk buying socks.

'I asked him, "What are you doing here?" All he said was, "You must go today, twelve o'clock. You must go today, twelve o'clock." That's all. I hurriedly asked around and found out that there was a big meeting of all branches of Buddhism from all over the world – Thailand, Japan, Taiwan, Singapore, Burma, Sri Lanka and Tibet. Because my legal hearing had been cancelled I had nothing to do, so I went along. It was a huge gathering with many people milling around. In a side room they were selling Buddhist artefacts, posters and books. I went in and there I found a table selling *Wisdom Energy*. I thought, "OK, that's my appointment." Incredible, you know. Each time it happened in just half a second.'

He told the woman selling the books that *Wisdom Energy*

mentioned a relative of his. She was more than interested since she was running the Paris office of the FPMT, the organization that Lama Yeshe had started. He asked if he could meet the two lamas who had meant so much to Zina. She told him that he had just missed Lama Zopa on his first-ever visit to France, but that Lama Yeshe was standing right behind him. He turned round and there on a wall was a large poster of Lama Osel.

'I said, "I don't understand." I didn't know anything about Buddhism. She laughed. Then she told me that Zina had had a very interesting life, that people said of her that she went to the Pure Lands of the Dakinis after she had died. I didn't know what all that meant, but it was interesting to me because I'd only heard about the bad side of Zina – taking drugs and things like that. The woman said, "It's not true, she did a great work. She was at the origin of a big movement of bringing Tibetan Buddhism to the West. She did a great job which was very beneficial. People pay her a lot of respect." I called my grandmother and she said it couldn't be true!'

Janine was pregnant by this time and the child inside her was impinging more and more on her and Gérard's life. It was at this point that they met the journalist who had actually interviewed Zina. He gave them his tapes and photographs of Zina in her mountain retreat twenty years earlier, telling them he had never once listened to the tapes.

'We went home,' said Gérard, 'and listened with great emotion to the voice. The tapes were bad quality, because they were so old. I began to think how strange it was that Zina was entering our lives in this way and that maybe she had a message of some sort to give to us. In the tapes she said she had some notes for a biography which she had given to someone. She said she couldn't get on with her writing because her practice was such that every day she saw things differently. So I thought maybe I should try and find this manuscript and do something with it. I thought that was the message she was trying to give us.

'I was thinking a lot about Zina, every day. Her life was

going on inside my life. I remember going to dinner and talking about my cousin, and the person from the next table leaning across and saying, "Are you talking about Zina? I knew her!" This sort of thing would happen every two or three days. Somebody knew her, or knew somebody who knew her. It was quite, quite strange.'

Then Gérard had a dream – a long and haunting dream which he remembers in precise detail to this very day. In it he was the guardian of a large sword which was in his grandmother's possession – a sword which gave off light like the sun. At this point in his account I recalled not only Yamantaka and his sword that Zina had been meditating on, but also the fact that when finding tulkus the Tibetans always ask prospective parents of any strong dreams they have had.

Gérard's task in his dream was to hide the sword from thieves who were coming in the night to steal it. Because the ground was covered in snow he knew the thieves would be able to follow his footsteps if he left, so he decided to make himself very small and post himself and the sword to Lama Zopa, whom at this stage he had never met. He duly put himself in an envelope, and when it arrived Lama Zopa was understandably astonished. He laughed and laughed – as he does in real life – and said happily, 'What a strange way to come here.'

Gérard continued the story of his prophetic dream: 'He asked me to follow him inside a very strange house which was totally white, no windows, just a very thin corridor and self-lighting. Afterwards I understood: it was a stupa. Lama Zopa went before me and in this thin corridor there was a little alcove with a beautiful crystal bell. It was an incredibly beautiful place, with exquisite light. Really divine – from another world. When I passed the bell it rang with a pure ringing sound. It was marvellous. Then Lama Zopa became quiet and said, "May I introduce you to Lama Yeshe." The bell was Lama Yeshe, whom, of course I had not met either.'

Two or three nights later Janine woke Gérard up in the

middle of the night. She was extremely agitated and was shouting: 'It's impossible! It's impossible! It can't be Zina because it's a boy. How is this? How can it be Zina? It's a boy!' she raged. Gérard was scared. Janine was drenched in sweat and her eyes were rolled back as though she were in a trance.

'I thought it best to leave her for a while. She quietened down and I woke her. I asked if she knew what she had been saying and she said she didn't remember anything. I repeated to her what she had been shouting, and she could see that something had happened because both she and the bed were soaked through.

'At this point I thought I had to get some advice from a lama or someone in authority, so I rang the woman I'd met at the Buddhist bookstall, who had become a friend. She called me back a few minutes later and told me that a high lama, the head of the Sakya sect of Tibetan Buddhism, was in Paris at that time. She'd spoken to him on my behalf, and he was happy to see me.'

In due course Gérard poured out to Sakya Trizin the whole curious sequence of events to date, including Janine's 'nightmare' message that the boy she was carrying in her womb was Zina. 'He told me that sometimes a meditator came back in the same family to go ahead, but that it was very rare, and auspicious. He also said that he would check to see if it were so, and asked me to come back the next day. So I did, and he told me the little boy Janine was carrying was Zina. He said he'd checked several times – because it was the first instance he'd ever come across of a reincarnation of a Westerner to a Westerner, but the results came out exactly the same. He added that he had met Zina in Darjeeling. She was special because she was the first Westerner to become a nun in the Gelugpa sect.'

In spite of the enormity of the news, Gérard was somehow not surprised. 'I knew it. For me, at that point it was just a confirmation. For months I had been totally in the mind of Zina. Listening to the tapes, trying to understand, I had the answer now. All that had happened was for this reason,' he said.

Janine also accepted the announcement with equanimity: 'I was a little surprised but didn't think it was crazy: I thought, "This is something, but I don't know what." I certainly didn't dismiss it. I was open to possibilities – no more, no less,' she said.

Later, His Holiness Sakya Trizin confirmed his findings in a letter that he sent to Lama Zopa. It read:

Dear Lama Zopa Rinpoche,
   This is an acknowledgement to your letter of 2nd August '90 as well as an official recognition for the reincarnation of your first Western disciple 'Zina'.
   As this is a case of recognition of reincarnation, it has taken quite some time to check again and again to verify the incarnation. Yes, the child (so-named) is the reincarnation of your first Western disciple Zina. To this effect, as in France, I checked several times and the conclusion came similar every time.
   With all my best wishes and prayers. Yours in the holy Dharma, (signed) His Holiness Sakya Trinzin (15th September 1990).

Nothing, however, could have prepared Janine and Gérard for the actual birth of the special child who had chosen them as parents. Janine had attended the births of several friends' babies and thought she knew what was in store. From the beginning, however, this birth was going to be radically different from anything she had ever seen or known. It was as though the new being that was once Zina was directing the whole event.

When the labour began Janine and Gérard went to the clinic, but the midwife who had prepared Janine was not there and the one on duty was not very sympathetic. Conveniently the pains stopped and Janine went home. Two days later the contractions started again and, although they thought it might be another false alarm, they set off for the clinic once more. Again the right midwife was not there, and again the pains stopped. Then the midwife arrived, the contractions started once more and the birth was under way.

Extraordinarily, Janine felt no pain, no discomfort, no fear. Quite the contrary. She was experiencing a state of extreme happiness, so much so that peals of laughter rang out. 'I was laughing so much that when Pierre came out he had a ring around his head which lasted for fifteen days. I kept thinking: "I wish all the women I knew could have births like this,"' she said.

Pierre had waited until the clock struck midnight. Then he emerged into this life making a sound like a chant. It was so loud that the doctors on the other side of the clinic heard it. 'It was like a humming noise, a tune, eerie, as if from another world,' recalls Gérard, trying to reproduce it. 'I remember it very well. It was really strange, you know. Everyone was a little bit frightened. He came out, with no crying. No crying at all. Just this loud sound. It was strange but profound.'

Then for a few seconds his heart stopped. The medical staff restarted it and told the parents not to worry, and that this sometimes happened. Then Pierre cried like a normal child. He was washed and given to his mother.

At this point the second amazing thing happened. When the midwife put Pierre on Janine's stomach he crossed his legs in the lotus position and sat there by himself unaided. He took his hands and made a very complicated gesture, like a Buddhist mudra, with all his fingers laced together, and looked at his mother like an old man. He did this without moving for some minutes. The whole event has been caught on video. Gérard, who was watching Janine's face, saw sheer terror.

'I had seen many births and knew that babies came out with floppy heads and weak bodies,' she said. 'Yet this was someone of my age, looking straight into my eyes, sitting there staring at me for about five minutes. I thought I had created a monster. I was frightened. Gérard was afraid I was not going to take the baby.'

The doctor arrived and couldn't believe what he was seeing. The nurse, with no idea of everything that had happened before, unconsciously blurted out: 'Oh look! A Tibetan monk.' As the doctor lifted the child up he commented that Pierre's eyes could follow and that his fingers could grasp, and that this too was unusual for a newborn baby.

Pierre came home and was a model baby. When he began to express himself it was in a sound like a mantra. 'Before he went to sleep he would take his thumb and mumble, like a monk repeating mantras,' recalled Gérard. Janine and I would listen behind the door. It was very nice. He was a very easy baby, never sick, never crying. Everyone who saw him became very happy. His development was always advanced for his age.'

In spite of his very unusual beginnings, Janine and Gérard have always attempted to give Pierre as normal a life as possible. Not for him the spotlight of the recognized tulku that has been meted out to Lama Osel. Pierre goes to a local school where no one pays him any particular attention, and this is exactly how his parents want it.

'The day Pierre tells me to my face, "My life is not this one, I have to do something else", then I will let him do it,' says Janine. 'But I don't want to influence him at all – he has so much within him. If it is inside him, it will come out.' I wondered if it would without the special education given to tulkus. Then I remembered Jetsunma, the woman in America who had developed her exceptional wisdom and compassion entirely of her own accord.

It is not that Gérard and Janine doubt what Sakya Trizin has told them – that their son is the reincarnation of Zina. Nor do they harbour any antipathy to or reluctance about Tibetan Buddhism. Quite the contrary. Although she is not a Buddhist, Janine has developed a strong respect for Lama Zopa and describes herself as being entirely 'open' to the religion's philosophies. She happily hangs in Pierre's bedroom the religious pictures that Lama Zopa sends him. When I saw

Gérard, he was involved in organizing the Dalai Lama's first visit to Paris. They are, they say, simply exercising caution and protecting their son from unwanted attention and the projections of others. It was, I thought, a typical Western approach. In the meantime, they wait and watch.

They observe many things that make them take notice. 'He has an unusual concern for others,' reported Janine. 'When he was two years old, for example, he was in a playground with other children and became extremely worried about a little girl who took her shoes off in case she got cold or hurt herself. I know that is not a usual attitude for a child his age. He worries about my smoking and is always telling me not to. He also has a highly developed moral sense. He corrects us if we say negative things about someone. He has a strong sense of right and wrong. I learn from him. He teaches me about things all the time.'

They say he learns very quickly and has a formidable memory. 'I can read him a story, and a week later if I read it again he'll know if I miss out a page. He can also tell you someone's name a year or more after he's heard it – long after I've forgotten,' his mother said.

At school he's a natural leader and, like Lama Osel, has enormous, powerful energy. 'It needs to be channelled because he wants to do everything at the same time. I have to be pretty tough with him – sometimes he has to be spanked. It's hard work. He has such a strong character that you can't make him do anything he doesn't want to.' Similarly, he doesn't like sleeping. 'It's crazy. I always have to argue with him about having a rest. He can have a late night but the next day he's never tired. He goes to bed at 8.30, and two hours later he's often awake,' said Janine.

She also notices that he likes responsibility. He loves getting his own breakfast and eating it by himself. He relishes being shown how to work machines and then doing it himself. He is also acutely aware of danger. He hates fighting and will never put himself at physical risk. 'He'll never dash out in front of open garages, nor pick up any bottles in the bathroom. I don't think I'm going to worry about him having a skateboard,' says Janine. I remarked that this characteristic was far away from the wild, risk-taking Zina. 'Maybe he is transformed,' Janine replied.

The most obviously striking feature about Pierre, however, is the way he speaks. He talks like an adult, using complex concepts and complicated words at the right moment. It's disarming, and people comment on it. 'He converses just like you and I. Our Buddhist friends say this is what truly sets him apart. I see all these things, but I decided from the beginning not to take too much notice of them in front of Pierre. I do not want him to be spoilt,' she added.

Another test came shortly after Sakya Trizin had recognized Pierre. Lama Zopa invited him, with his parents, to Kopan. If Pierre was the reincarnation of Zina, this would well and truly be a homecoming, for Kopan was where Zina had spent her first spiritually charged days as a Buddhist nun. Kopan had changed radically since the days when Zina and her lamas had gone to live there and started teaching those early Western seekers in the 1960s. New buildings had sprung up, water had been conducted up the hill, a dining room had been built, a splendid new gompa had been erected – even showers and lavatories had been installed.

Immediately Pierre arrived he began to act differently. He went to a box and started to pull out religious objects and different types of robes. His parents protested, but Lama Zopa laughed and said Pierre was merely doing his own 'practice'. He also remarked that Pierre had the same 'energy' as Zina. He was then shown the gompa, but insisted it was his 'house'. Day after day as he walked past the gompa he would say it was his 'house'. Later his parents found out that the present gompa had been built on the site of the house where Zina had lived.

On another occasion they visited the famous nearby Buddhist temple at Swayambuth. Suddenly Gérard and Janine realized that it was very quiet. Pierre was no longer with them. They rushed off to look for him, and found him quite alone doing full-length prostrations in front of a statue of the Buddha. When he realized he had been discovered he was furious – his cover had been blown! He was just two and a half years old at the time.

This display of ostensibly wanting to have nothing to do with the outer trappings of Tibetan Buddhism continued. 'He wouldn't accept the katags, the white scarves which people offered him. He wouldn't sit by Lama Zopa. Anything the monks wanted him to do he'd say "no" to, very strongly and loudly. In the end they called him "Mr No".

'What was fascinating, though, was that although he didn't want to have anything to do with the monks, he showed a great affinity to the nuns. He had very good rapport with them. He called them his friends. Personally, I don't know how he told the difference,' commented Janine.

During the time Pierre was at Kopan there was an official recognition to which three hundred people were invited. Lama Osel's robes were brought out for him to wear but he promptly refused to put them on. At a certain moment, however, he changed his mind. 'He said, "OK." And suddenly he was transformed – the way he wore those robes, the way he moved in them. It was beautiful. Suddenly I saw my child completely,' said Janine.

But although Janine was developing a deepening respect for Lama Zopa and some of the people she met at Kopan, she wanted to make her position absolutely clear. 'I told Lama Zopa that when Pierre tells me himself that he wants to teach, them he can have him. Until that time I want my son to have an ordinary life with us in France.'

Lama Zopa concurred. 'He's your child. I do not want to take him from you. Just take great care of him, be careful whom he mixes with and the environment you put him in,' was all he said.

For people who were not brought up as Buddhists and had not sought out Buddhism of their own accord (like the parents of other Western tulkus), finding themselves with a child who has been declared a tulku has been something of a challenge for Janine and Gérard. Since Pierre's birth they have struggled to understand what reincarnation is and what it means, in particular, for their son.

'I feel really convinced that Pierre has some particle of Zina,' said Janine. 'I know by the way he behaves. But I don't think Zina "became" Pierre. I hated it when people began to come to see him and say, "Oh, Zina." He became a curiosity. It was too much of a show and so I stopped it. Lama Zopa has said that Pierre has the same energy as Zina, but I never met Zina and so it's difficult to say. But I am completely at peace with the situation, and have no fears,' she added.

Gérard, with his lawyer's mind, has conscientiously researched the meaning of rebirth both within the Tibetan tulku system and within modern physics. He is fascinated by the meeting-point between the two streams of thought and follows each new development closely. He thinks it is of vital importance to know exactly who his son is. As a result he has developed strong and individual views on the subject.

'Reincarnation is not one person living in another person's body. It's not that at all. That's the Western point of view, the Christian perspective which says there is a body and a soul which lives in that body. That's not true. The mind is everywhere in the body, and everywhere else also. It is not as simple as moving into a house and living there.

'When people began to say, "Oh, this is Zina", I thought it was my duty to know what was going on, in order to be knowledgeable and to protect Pierre. I read many books, and discovered that the Tibetans themselves are divided into a lot of ways of explaining the matter. And on the other side you have the scientific research, especially physics, which has some good explanations.'

In the end he bows down to the enormity of the phenomenon he is facing: 'Actually, the continuation of consciousness is something totally outside of our "channel". It is not possible to reflect on it as if it were in our "channel", because it is quite "out" of it,' he said.

For all the intellectual debate, his son is flesh and blood and, as Gérard is the first to concede, his own experience with Pierre has not been found in books. They have a loving and dynamic relationship.

'From the time he was two months old he looked at me with *la reconnaissance*. He did not exactly pay homage, but there was gratitude for something. It was in his eyes. "I am Pierre and I thank you." I saw that very often, before he was able to speak. It is like a great confidence given to parents. And I think truly Zina achieved her commitment which was to come back. Before he was born I had a feeling of Zina as she was in the photos. I felt her presence. At the moment of Janine's "nightmare" this image disappeared completely. And when Pierre came and was only able to speak with the eyes, I refound that same image, that same feeling, through him.'

It all seemed so convincing, but for me one over-riding question remained unanswered. Why had Zina reincarnated in a male form? The feminist in me baulked at the notion that Zina, the exotic, wild, strong, determined and courageous woman who had achieved so much as a female, had forsaken her gender to prove her spiritual prowess as a man. In the patriarchal world of Tibetan Buddhism, we badly needed female figures of reverence and awe to look up to, to emulate. To become a boy seemed a terrible betrayal of her sex.

'If you read the scriptures with a superficial eye, you will see that there is a commitment for the nuns to become monks in their future lives. Personally, I take that on the energy level only, not the body level,' commented Gérard.

'But when you actually examine Tibetan society you can find high nuns who have been reborn as high nuns. So, everybody has their own special way. If you look at Zina's credibility, it was not 100 per cent. Many of the people who knew her simply can't accept that she became a very high nun with an advanced practice. They don't believe she could change so fast. The fact that it's not a female now, but it's a boy, makes the difference so clear,' he said.

It was a logical explanation, but my disappointment remained.

But what of the future? To accept that your child is the reincarnation of a high spiritual practitioner is one thing, but what to do with that knowledge is another. Putting a child like Pierre on the right educational and spiritual track is a particularly heavy duty and, more than most parents, Janine and Gérard have a right to wonder what Pierre is going to become when he grows up.

Janine has no preconceptions at all. 'Anything can happen. I'm not scared. I'm open to whatever arises,' she said. Gérard, however, has sought practical advice on how to deal with the huge responsibility he now finds himself with.

'I have asked a lot of different lamas which way Pierre might go, and what I should do. I spent seven hours with Lama Zopa discussing it, and it was very interesting. But the answer is always the same: "Wait and see." One high lama said that, because Pierre is a tulku, if we don't take care of him he could become "crazy". Another said that Pierre would do a lot of things for the benefit of beings. All of them said that things would appear more clear when Pierre is seven or eight, and that it would come from him.'

Sometimes, however, Pierre makes little remarks which stop Gérard in his tracks. 'The other day his grandmother was talking to him and asked where I was. Pierre said I was in my office, which he knows very well. She then asked, "Where is that?" and he replied: "Kathmandu." Sometimes he asks me when I am going back to Kopan. So one never knows,' he finished, laughing.

In the meantime Janine and Gérard, like all parents, simply try to do their best for their child by giving him every opportunity they can to develop as a rounded human being. 'I also try to learn as much as I can about Tibetan Buddhism, to direct him, if necessary. My experience with these very old traditions like martial arts and now Buddhism has shown me that it is important to understand why we are here, what for, who we are. And later, you learn to act for the benefit of others. That's the other side. It's mostly a matter of knowledge of the true nature of things.

'There is no pressure. Why should there be? There is only pressure in things that need to be done now, like education, setting limits, learning how to say "thank you". Basic things.

'Personally I think it will happen – but not in a monk's way. In Kopan he showed us that he did not want to have anything to do with monks – he did not want to sit on the throne, did not want to get dressed up in robes.

'In the future he will determine for himself what he is going to do. In the end the question is not the job, or the way of life. The question is knowledge. In that way I think my job is to give him the opportunity to reach the goal that he has set himself – whatever that is,' said Gérard.

And the rest of us who knew about the remarkable Zina can only wait.

8

TRINLEY TULKU

Having said goodbye to Pierre and his parents in Paris, I took the train on what was essentially another mystery journey. There was a French tulku, I had heard, living in a Tibetan monastery in the great mountain ranges behind the southern coast, but he had rigorously eschewed publicity of any sort. I had got his name, Trinley Tulku, from the followers of the Nygma sect and as fate would have it I had met a man in Paris who kindly gave me the tulku's telephone number. A pleasant, young voice had answered the call, and much to my amazement had said I could at least come and meet him.

In my experience all journeys with a serious spiritual intent present obstacles and hindrances of monumental proportions, as though to test the sincerity of your purpose. This pilgrimage was no exception.

The Friday night traffic around Paris was horrendous. While my taxi stayed in its jam my intended train left. I waited in the queue at the Gare de Lyon for over an hour as the new-fangled computerized ticketing procedure took twenty minutes to find and sell each person their fare. When eventually my turn came there was only one seat available in the train I needed – in the smoking compartment. Nightmare. But I took it.

However, the fumes and the hassle grew less as the train went deeper into the French countryside. The super-fast TGV finally gave way to a rickety suburban train which deposited me at a picturesque station in a small town near Grenoble. I sat outside the café in the cobbled station square, waiting for the lift which was to take me to Trinley Tulku. Surrounded by tubs of geraniums I drank my glass of wine, listening to the evening songbirds and watching the sun set behind the rustic ochre buildings, contemplating that this was what I dreamed about when, far away, I thought of France. An old Deux Chevaux duly arrived and its driver propelled us like a maniac virtually on two hubcaps up the steep, winding mountain road, carried away on an outpouring of exhaust and loud jazz from the car radio. He was one of the regular visitors to the monastery and he came for the peace, he told me.

When the engine and radio were eventually silenced as we arrived at my destination, I conceded that he was right. Here at this Franco-Tibetan monastery perched on the edge of a great mountain, there was indeed a powerful stillness and a breathtaking beauty. On the ground, there were wild flowers everywhere – blue, white, red and yellow – while all around were soaring vistas. Later I was told that wild deer roamed the wooded slopes, which seemed most auspicious since the deer is the national emblem of Tibet. The monastery itself was a reflection of the two cultures it embodied. Here and there were the original buildings – lovely old stone cottages with ramshackle slate roofs, looking like the homes of French cowherds. Above them was a new, large, white temple, rising strong and square in true Tibetan fashion.

Trinley Tulku came to meet me. In the evening twilight I saw a tall, slim young man in maroon and gold robes, with one of the gentlest, kindest smiles I had ever seen. His eyes beamed welcome as he took me in to the monastery kitchen for a cup of tea. He was, he said by way of conversation, learning to drive and was about to take his test. He was looking forward to getting behind the wheel, and I reflected that, no matter how remote the place, how strange the lifestyle, the tracks of modern Western life are never far away. He spoke good English with a French accent underlaid with American tones, reflecting his background. His father was French and his mother American – that was the sum of what I knew about Trinley Tulku, the rinpoche who had been kept a secret.

The next morning, sitting cross-legged on the floor of his room at the top of the temple with its panoramic views over the valleys and mountains beyond, Trinley Tulku told me as much of his story as he was prepared to divulge. He had been born in 1975 to parents who were already followers of Tibetan Buddhism, and so was brought into contact with the lamas.

'When I was very little I very much wanted to become a monk. I kept asking my mother to take me to the monastery. I loved it when I put on monk's robes. There are pictures of me smiling, always smiling, as a small child in monk's robes. Yet I remember when my mother finally left me at the monastery I was very sad. For a few days I cried. It was natural. It was the first time I had been without my mother and I was so young. She used to come and see me often. Then I got used to being in the monastery – I knew she'd come again.' The same warmth and extraordinary sweetness that I had seen the night before were still there in this eighteen-year-old rinpoche with the open face and the soft smiling eyes. He told me he had been a monk since he was three years old.

Like most of the other Western tulkus, Trinley's recognition had come about through his parents' own involvement with the Buddha dharma. At eighteen months he could speak Tibetan, learnt from his Tibetan nanny – an invaluable tool for the life he was destined to follow. While playing around the Buddha centre he had caught the eye of Kalu Rinpoche, who after the usual checks officially recognized him as the reincarnation of someone called Khashap Rinpoche. This recognition was formally ratified by none other than HH the Karmapa – a figure who generates almost as much reverence among Tibetan Buddhists as does the Dalai Lama, especially among the Kagyu sect.

'I was told I was the reincarnation of this lama called Khashap Rinpoche, who had had a monastery in Tibet. I don't know much about the story except that he died quite young in India from TB. He was in retreat when he died, and I am supposed to be his reincarnation,' Trinley Tulku said. He gave little away, although whether this was because he didn't know, didn't want to tell, or simply was reluctant to talk about any spiritual prowess he might possess was hard to tell. I pressed for a little more information.

'In my previous life I wanted to come to the West, and apparently said to those around me that we would all meet again in the West. Otherwise I don't remember much about when I was young, except that the Karmapa and Kalu Rinpoche liked me. The Kharmapa right away gave me refuge,' he said, meaning the acceptance of a person into the Buddhist faith.

In fact his early years were spent by the side of Kalu Rinpoche, who nurtured and fostered the spiritual potential that lay within him. It must have been an extraordinary life for the little Franco-American boy, living like the son of a great spiritual adept, learning from him the rich and complex lessons and rituals of Tibetan Buddhism. Those who saw him at this time say he used to run in and out of the ceremonies looking completely at home, and Kalu Rinpoche was always loving, always doting, sometimes indulging, like a fond father. While some say Trinley Tulken was exceptional in the way he would help Kalu Rinpoche in the ceremonies, others reported that he was rather wild and somewhat out of control.

'I was with Kalu Rinpoche for seven years travelling with him in Europe and South-East Asia,' he told me, 'visiting the Karmapa's centres there. And when I was ten I came to here to France.'

This was when his serious training started. For eight years now, day in day out, he has deligently led the disciplined life of a Tibetan monk, following much the same pattern as millions of others before him in those highly organized seats of spiritual learning high in the Himalayas. To say that his daily timetable is demanding would be an understatement.

He awakes at 6 a.m. and does his personal practice. At 7 a.m. he goes to puja, the morning prayer ceremony, with the other residents. Breakfast follows at 8 a.m. Then he studies with his teacher until 12.30, which is lunchtime. From 3 p.m. to 5 p.m. he does more studies in English. At 5 p.m. he does homework until 7 p.m., when he attends another puja. At 8 p.m. he eats supper. From 9 p.m. until 11.30 p.m. he does more ritual practices and homework. Then he goes to bed.

There is no break on Saturday or Sunday, Tibetans having no notion of a weekend. This rigorous routine of learning, praying and meditating continues year-round, non-stop! And Trinley Tulku himself is utterly determined that it will continue for as long as it takes for his geshe degree to be complete. And that could be another ten years.

He doesn't mind. This tulku, Western though he is, is taking the traditional Tibetan route, albeit with French and English studies included. 'I will continue studying for a long time. I want to complete them. It's stupid to stop. I believe this is a very good opportunity,' he declared softly.

I asked him what he wanted to do with this life.

'First of all I want to help His Holiness the Karmapa and Kalu Rinpoche. That's my main job – after all, they recognized me,' he answered, knowing full well that those great Tibetan lamas who had recognized him had passed away and were now in new bodies as eminent young masters, going through much the same training as he himself was under-taking. His answer, though, was somewhat disappointing. It seemed as though Trinley was talking like an obedient Tibetan monk who had been well versed in the Eastern notion of filial piety above all. Had he been brainwashed into merely continuing the system as it stood? Had his Western capacity for creative lateral thinking, that streak of individuality which is bred in us, been totally dissipated? Was this all he had been born for? He went on:

'Then maybe, if I can help European people to understand Buddhism, I would like to do that. It's new here, and most people don't understand the real dharma. They like funny things like the paintings, the thrones, the religious objects. But the Buddhist philosophy, which can make a profound difference to your life – that I would like to explain,' he said.

The disappointment vanished. Here it was again, stated

loud and clear – the purpose of the new Western tulku, the reason why a Tibetan sage should choose to be born into a foreign land, into a foreign body. Why else should this be happening if not to tell the world about the secrets of that highly evolved, mystical path which promises to sever all beings ultimately from their chains of sorrow, and which flourishes in that icy stronghold of Tibet?

And so, if Trinley Tulku's chosen life seemed at first glance to be nothing more than a returning to the conventional life of a Tibetan lama, his own intention was far greater. Later I saw from a brochure that he has in fact started to teach at the monastery. He directs meditation sessions and explains the rudimentary practice in the great Tibetan deities. But as he says himself, he is still learning from his own Tibetan teacher, and there is a long way to go.

For ten years now Trinley Tulku has been on his mountain in southern France, keeping to his extraordinarily rigorous daily timetable – an isolated, austere existence for a boy who has just become a young man. Doesn't he miss parties, football and the other things that people of his age usually enjoy? Does he ever leave his mountain?

'I don't do any sport,' he replied. 'After lunch I go for walks, to get outside. Sometimes I go for trips to my father's house, and I go to the cinema sometimes with my friends who live here. I don't really have much time! You must remember I was put into this when I was very young. My life is happy. The only thing I wish to do is to be able to study more, to know more. I don't actually like studying, you understand, but I like to know things, so I persevere. Knowledge is important – not to make you better than anyone else, but to make life happier. Wisdom helps, whatever age you are,' he said, and I noted the book lying beside him, a hefty tome titled *L'Art de Penser*, which he told me explained the basis of European philosophy. It had been recommended to him by a professor in Paris who takes an interest in him. 'It's a nice book,' he added. He reads a lot of mathematics too, as well as French and English literature.

Later, a resident who had been at the monastery for some years told me that Trinley Tulku was indeed very bright. 'When he came here as a small boy he was very wild, out of control. But the lama who has taken care of him here is both very strong and very loving. Those two things together changed him. He said we were to ignore the tulku and address the child. It is a very healthy attitude. He needed that, not the reverence.

'But from the start we could see that he was very clever and extremely mature. He is also deeply dedicated to the dharma, and the dharma qualities of sweetness and kindness are natural to him. They have always been there.'

Finally I asked Trinley the question I put to all the Western tulkus: did he feel any connection with his predecessor? The answer was surprisingly similar.

'I don't think I'm exactly the same person. It's like this. Everything is changing constantly. For instance, I don't get older at my birthday. You can't see me getting older, day by day, but in ten years' time I will look older. But each day, each second I am getting older. Everything is impermanent. Even "I" doesn't exist. The way things exists is very complex,' he said. I remembered the teachings I had received over the years – that nothing has any inherent self-existence and that our sense of an "I" is as non-substantial as everything else in our universe. In this way what Trinley Tulku was saying was right. He could not be exactly the same as Khashap Rinpoche. Khashap Rinpoche was as ephemeral as the young man sitting before me.

He continued: 'We are all pushed by a karma, but tulkus are often born to help sentient beings. They are not reborn just through the force of their karma.'

It was all he would say, but it was enough. What he had alluded to was what is written in the holy texts: that the bodhisattva does not have to come back to earth to pay off debts and reap the experiences that have been sown in countless other lifetimes. The bodhisattva has found the way out. The only reason for returning to this world of sorrows is to be of service to others.

I had been let into the intensely private world of Trinley Tulku, and was grateful for the glimpse I had been given. As I set off down the mountain in another unpredictable car, this diligent, gentle rinpoche with an exceptionally well-developed sense of responsibility and a broad smile waved me goodbye. I wondered where his life would lead when and if he ever came down from the mountain.

9

DR DENNING

Dr Hazel Denning first came to my attention one lazy week-day afternoon in Sydney when I switched on the television to find Oprah Winfrey, the American chat show host, masterminding a heated debate on past lives. In her audience was an elderly, intelligent and extremely eloquent woman with a string of degrees to her name, who had founded the Association for Past-Life Research and Therapies. As a pioneer in this type of work she had travelled the world giving lectures and seminars on her topic.

Apart from speaking with impressive lucidity and integrity on the matter of past lives and their impact on present time, Dr Denning interested me because she was also a highly qualified clinical psychologist. Her informed contribution to the ever-growing dossier of information about reincarnation and its implications for modern Western life would, I judged, be invaluable to me.

I was not disappointed. At a small airport in southern California I was met by a slim, erect and sprightly woman who, in spite of her advancing years (she was well into her eighties), drove with alarming confidence to Riverside, home of the Californian orange, where she lives and has her headquarters. Around the walls of her bungalow were the many certificates and degrees that she has collected during her long, inquisitive life: the two PhDs, the two Masters, the Bachelors, as well as numerous documents proclaiming her proficiency in the fields of hypnosis and parapsychological studies.

During the two days that I was with her, Dr Denning

described her work to me and told me how she had come to be doing it. 'From the time I was very small I was looking for the "why" and the reason for the pain and suffering. I didn't buy that God "just put it on us". That didn't make any sense to me.'

Then when she was in her twenties she came across her first book on reincarnation. 'I thought, "Wow, I've found the answers I've been looking for!" I was absolutely euphoric. I thought, "At last I've found something that makes sense, that explains all these inequalities.

'At first I was hesitant to accept it completely. So I read everything I could lay my hands on to see if the idea of reincarnation was true. I read all the ancient stuff and discovered that all the great religions taught it. It was even in Christianity until 533, when the Roman Emperor and his wife outlawed it. Two Popes were actually killed trying to keep it in! Not many people know that. Nor do they know that the early Church Fathers like Origen and St Augustine also believed in reincarnation. So all those who say that reincarnation is contrary to Christianity just don't know what they're talking about!' she asserted.

'Then I read that some of the greatest minds in all ages also believed in reincarnation – people like Plato, Aristotle and Socrates down through Henry Ford, Gladstone, Thomas Edison, General Patton and many more. All this made it a lot easier for me to accept,' she said. It was simply a matter of time before Dr Denning incorporated her vast study of reincarnation into her practice as a qualified psychotherapist in order to help make people well.

One of the most burning questions I had to ask was how she reconciled the two seemingly opposing strands of her professional life – the conventional psychotherapist and the past-life regressionist. How did she accommodate the current psychotherapeutic rule that it is events in *this* life that are the main causes of our problems with the ancient laws of karma – that we basically bring everything on ourselves? They were questions which, I admitted, still bothered me.

'I never did believe that environment was the most important factor in people's behaviour – not that environment
doesn't have a bearing, of course!' she said emphatically.
'What I believe is that the purpose of life, here on earth, is
spiritual evolvement, and that when we come into this life we
have things we have to work on, problems that we have not
resolved in previous lives. A child may come in with anger
or joy – and the things that happen in that life may modify
what is already there. Let me put it this way. I think that the
destiny or purpose of a person cannot be changed, but parents
and the environment can make it easier or more difficult for
that person to work on his or her problems.'

Hazel Denning duly became a qualified hypnotist, the
means by which she would lead people to re-experience lives
that they had led earlier. With this she was as meticulous in
her search for honesty as in all her endeavours. She was not
going to control people's minds in any way.

'In the early days they taught us post-hypnotic suggestion.
You know the sort of thing – "You are not going to eat. Food
is repulsive to you" – which I was not going to do. It was
totally against my principles. I found a process where I could
use the method without this manipulation. I prefer the term
"altered state" to "hypnosis",' she explained.

In 1980 she set up the Association for Past-Life Research
and Therapies, and since then has watched the movement
increase beyond her wildest expectations as interest and
belief in reincarnation have accelerated remarkably. She stated
categorically that past-life therapy is now one of the most
powerful tools available for transformation in the fields of
integrative medicine (which aims to treat the whole person,
mind and body) and psychology. 'We grew fast not only here
but overseas as well. I was invited to speak on reincarnation
on several occasions both in Asia and at Utrecht University
in Holland, one of the oldest universities in the world and
one of the first to have a chair in parapsychology,' she said.

Back at home, the people who come to her are drawn from
all walks of life. She uses a mixture of regular therapy and

past-life regression. 'When regular therapy doesn't answer the problem, then just a dip into the past will do it,' she says. Her clients cover the broad spectrum of American society. 'I get ministers of the Church, professional people, a lot of teachers, people in the military, ordinary men and women. The thing a lot of them want to know is "What is the purpose of my life?", "What am I doing here?", "What have I come here for this time?"'

Most of the people who come to see her fall into the thirty-to-forty age group, although she has regressed a child as young as nine. 'It was a girl. She wanted to come of her own accord, and got her parents' permission to do so. She was exceptionally mature. She came because she wanted to know about her fear of blood. Almost as soon as we began she saw herself as an old man, very weak and doddery on his deathbed. She was apparently dying of a heart attack. Then she stopped and said, "No, I'm dying of a broken heart." She went on to describe how, as the man in her previous life, she had taken "her" wife out to dinner. During the evening a man had come into the restaurant with a gun and mown down several people, including "her" wife. She saw the wife die in a pool of blood – and had carried over the horror into her present life, along with a feeling of guilt that somehow she should have taken better care of "her" wife,' Dr Denning recounted.

Her views, stated clearly and with considerable authority, stem from witnessing literally thousands of hours of people's past-life dramas. During the time I spent with her she regaled me with story upon story of people who had been transformed by her work – and the theories that she has subsequently developed from it. Our conversation was, I thought, not only informative but also highly entertaining.

VM: Why are people reborn?
HD: When I take a person into an altered state, if they are having a problem in this life I ask them to go back to before they were born and see why they chose these particular parents and what their purpose is in coming back. Through

the years the answer is nearly always, 'I really don't want to come back. Getting into a body is like going to prison. It's really confined.' I then say, 'Well, why do you come back, because no one is making you?' And the answer is always 'Because the earth is a classroom, a school where we have to learn as personalities. If I want to grow spiritually I have to go back. And I do want to grow spiritually.' That's the answer I get from people in altered states.

VM: From your experience, how many times do you think people live on this earth?

HD: As many times as it takes for them to learn the lessons they are working on. Even in this life people sometimes take years to grasp the meaning of their problem.

I have one woman, for instance, who the first time she came to me said, 'I'm here to learn to love.' As a psychologist, how do you teach someone to love? To say you've got to love to get love doesn't tell you anything, really.

I worked with that woman for about eighteen years before she found it. Not all the time. There would be years when I wouldn't see her. In the interim she'd have a marriage, then a live-in, then another marriage, then five or six live-ins! She called me one day and said she couldn't stand it any more. She was going to come every day until she found the answer. She finally saw herself in Greece as a young girl of about fourteen, in love with a boy who worked around their establishment. Her father, who was very wealthy, found out and was furious. He sent the boy out to an island and sold his daughter to an older man. She was so angry and upset that she committed suicide. When she died she said, 'I will never, never, never love again.'

I've discovered from doing this work that the last thought we have when we die, if it's a negative one, is what we come back with. If we die in a rage, for instance, hating and resentful, then we come back and have to start working on that.

After her discovery, this woman found a beautiful man,

married him and had two lovely children. She is still married and says she never dreamed she could experience such happiness.

Following this case I concluded that some people are not ready to solve something right off. They have to work through a lot of stuff before they are ready to emerge with the answer. I've also learnt that you can't fool your own mind. Unless you find the right thing it doesn't work. Often I have to go back and back a number of times before we find what I call the core issue, which is the key to the problem.

VM: Sceptics would say that your patients are conjuring up images and stories from their subconscious to explain and justify their pain and unhappiness.

HD: Then why doesn't psychotherapy work with these people? Because it doesn't. I've had lots of clients who have been in psychotherapy for a number of years, and their problems have not been mitigated in the least. And if their minds were that clever to make up stuff they would have done it a long time ago, I would have thought.

VM: Do you think we actively choose the kinds of lives we live?

HD: Absolutely! Let me tell you a really hairy story. This woman came to me and said, 'My mother is dying, my father is already dead, and both of them abused me sexually from the time I was three until I was thirteen.' She went into an altered state straight away and started reliving her trauma. She began screaming, 'Daddy, please, please don't hurt me any more, Daddy!' She went on to say, 'I don't want my mother to die without forgiving her, but I'm having trouble because I hated them both.'

Now, if someone wants to forgive and wants to stop hating, then they've reached quite a high stage of spiritual evolution and can be helped. If, on the other hand, someone starts saying, 'Don't talk to me about forgiving those goddam bastards – I'll never forgive them, I hate their guts', then there's no point pursuing it. They're not ready.

But with this lady I thought, 'How do I help someone forgive parents who have done *that* to them?' But she went back into a past life and saw that she had been a kid in Germany, a street child, who had killed another child and then had been taken to Auschwitz to ensure that the babies being killed in the camp were really dead. At first the work didn't worry her, but eventually she couldn't take it any more, tried to escape and was shot.

She said, 'When I came back I decided to choose parents who would abuse me so that I could get rid of my karma in a big hurry.' She added that she should thank them both for being instruments through which she could pay off her karmic debts.

VM: Have you ever tried to verify the past-life stories that you have heard?

HD: I have checked wherever I can. There was a woman who had an unreal obsession about her children visiting sideshows. She was adamant that they stayed away, even though she knew it was unreasonable. In her altered state she went back to when she was a 'fat lady' in a show and hated it. She got the name of the woman and the name of the town. It happened that a man in the same group knew the town, and he volunteered to check it out when he was next there. Sure enough, at the beginning of this century, there had been a fat lady of that name in the circus that she named. Incidentally, in her present life this woman also had a weight problem.

There was also a woman who recalled going down with the *Titanic*. She was a businessman in that life. She got the name and later checked it out with the official records. Sure enough, she found her name. It gave her a very strange feeling, she said.

Apart from this physical checking, the real proof is that the stories my clients come up with seem to 'fit', and when discovered can bring about real change.

VM: Do people ever feel guilty rather than relieved

when they see the negative things they have done in their past lives?

HD: Not when they understand the process and the purpose. I tell people it doesn't matter what happened to you, it's not important. It's only what you learn from it. I believe that's the principle.

One case I had was very interesting. A woman came into my office. She sat down and started banging the arms of the chair and screaming at the top of her lungs: 'I hate God! Jesus Christ is a fraud! I've done everything. I've gone to therapy. I've read the Bible all the way through. But nothing helps.' Everything had gone wrong in her life, in spite of the fact that she was very capable. She'd build up businesses but they would fall apart. Her marriage was a mess. Physically she looked like an old woman. Her doctor had told her that her body was twenty years older than her chronological age.

We went to work on it. Eventually she saw herself as a cardinal in the Inquisition, putting people on the rack. This was deeply upsetting to her. She knew it was wrong, but it was what the Church demanded. I asked her to see the reason why she was a powerful instrument in the Inquisition, and she replied, much to her surprise, 'It was to revolutionize the Catholic Church because it was so corrupt. I was given that responsibility.' I've discovered through the years that many of the horrible things that people do are for a purpose.

VM: Karma becomes extremely intricate when you begin to look at it in this perspective, doesn't it? I mean, are perpetrators of what we would call wicked deeds actually blameless when you consider that they are merely providing the means for a person to get his karmic pay-back?

HD: I believe that the system is so intricate and so perfect that we serve each other's needs. The simplest way to explain it is in terms of the sadist and the masochist. You know perfectly well that a sadist has to be with a masochist because that is their emotional need.

There is never any fault. Every experience is a teaching. You discover that you are a perpetrator in one life and a victim in another. With some people this goes on for a number of lives until they get the point.

I believe we choose everything – including the painful lives we have. When we can discover and accept the purpose of the kind of lives we have, then things can change. If a person can take responsibility they can solve almost anything. I can't help people who blame, or those whose ego-strength is too weak to accept that responsibility. They're not ready. As therapists we have to recognize that.

At the ultimate level the soul has knowledge of the whole process – knows who you are, why you are here, what you've done, what you're going to do and all the rest. But it's the personality that has to learn the lessons – for some reason which I don't know. I don't make the rules, I only interpret them.

Then some people choose not to change. One woman, who had terrible eyesight and wore real thick glasses, saw that she chose to have bad eyes in order not to be so materialistic and self-centred and to begin to look inwards. After that she was happy with her near-blindness, and didn't want to give it up.

VM: Do you find people get drawn back to the same people over and over again?

HD: Yes. And the relationships change. Sometimes people come back together to solve things. Other times we come back just to help people. I think some of the great martyrs chose to be martyrs – to lift the consciousness of mankind. So many people have the wrong idea about karma – they think it is only punishment. It isn't at all. It's cause and effect.

I knew a woman who was a doctor – a lovely person who was married to the sourest man I'd ever met. He was constantly blaming and nagging her. It was incredible how cruel he was, without meaning to be. She had gradually withdrawn emotionally from him, but she would never leave him. One day she had a past-life regression and saw herself meeting this man in another time, and he was a lost soul. She promised him she would marry him in the next life and help him find himself.

After that she really turned on the love. She had a totally different feeling towards him, and within a year he was a changed man – he was going to church with her, he drove around town in a red sports car, he became fun and developed a sense of humour.

I love this story. I use it with the wives and families of alcoholics who are tolerating the drinker but have withdrawn their feelings. I tell them, 'If you can take the irritation out of your voice, if you can really care and express it, then he'll change.' I've known a few wives who were strong enough to do that.

VM: Is there a set period of time between dying and coming back?

HD: Some people come back within hours. Those who've died on battlefields, for example, can't handle being out of the body. I think that's the reason for the increase in population after wars. Others stay away for hundreds of years. I believe many people coming back now haven't been here since the Atlantean Age – they had to wait until what they knew began to be acceptable here. They came back to help bring in the New Age.

VM: Have you ever come across people who have lived in other planets or dimensions?

HD: Sometimes. There are quite a few who believe that earth is the lowest planet in the totem pole! I've had some clients who said they came from another planet. There was one man who wrote in another script and then translated it. It was very interesting. He came from a totally different culture. He also understood the simultaneity principle – of the past, present and future all happening right now. It's very hard for me to understand.

VM: Have you discovered any of your own past lives?

HD: Oh, yes. My previous life was an extremely cold

one. I was a woman in England, married to a diplomat, and ran one of those lovely homes with lots of servants and parties and so forth. But there was no love in my life. When I died in all my neck ruffles with my servants tiptoeing around I remember holding my sister's hand and saying, 'If I had my life to live over, I would love more.'

In this present life I lost a sister when I was eleven and she was nine. I grieved for two years. I needed to do that to be able to feel again.

The most dramatic experience, however, happened when I was in the shower. From the time I was in eighth grade I had a liver problem. I'd get these terrible bilious spells with awful headaches and nausea. I suffered horribly. I also used to have a terrible temper. As an adult I broke blood vessels in my neck twice due to rage. I'd get so angry at times that I felt the top of my head was going to blow right off! But nobody would ever know it, because I controlled it.

One day about ten years ago I was standing in the shower with a headache and I said, very firmly and loudly, 'God, I want to know the reason for these liver problems. Why do I have them?'

It was instantaneous. I saw myself on a battlefield as a crusader with gauntlets on and a spear through my liver. I was in an absolute rage for dying for a cause I no longer believed in. I hated what we were doing – the burning and destroying of beautiful temples – but there was nothing I could do about it. I was dying and would never see my wife and two sons again. I died in anger – and my liver became a symbol for that rage.

In the shower a little voice said, 'That's where your rage comes from.' I've never had a bilious attack since.

VM: Has belief in past lives helped you live your present life?

HD: Knowing what I know, I have never grieved. The other dimension is as real to me as this one. My mother, husband and son all died very close together, and I didn't grieve for any of them. The day my son died in a motorbike accident I went on to give a university lecture that had been organized. Afterwards the professor was profoundly shocked and asked how I could have done such a thing. I replied, 'Well, you think it's a tragedy, but I don't. And that's the difference.'

I knew my son's past – that he had been a monk in his previous three lives, and he had come this time to find out how the world was. He lived very dangerously. I knew he didn't want to continue to live like that, so he chose to leave before he did anything really bad. While I was sorry it had happened, because I had the normal visions of him growing up to be a fine citizen and all those things, I was glad that he was gone because he was in so much pain.

Similarly, my husband died one morning on the tennis court. After I heard, I went into the study to ring the family – and I never had a more transcendental experience in my life. The whole room lit up – it was charged with energy. The hair on my arms stood up and I felt euphoric. Totally euphoric. It was as if he just wrapped me in his love and said, 'Honey, I did it just the way I wanted to.' Again, I went to a board meeting that night. After the business was done I told everyone and they were distraught. I had to go round comforting them.

I can help people with their grieving, but I get distressed at people's over-grieving. There's often guilt somewhere if that happens.

VM: What you are saying is that everything happens for a purpose. Do you believe that ultimately it's for the good?

HD: Absolutely. Yes, absolutely! I think that's the divine plan. I believe that we are literally God expressing. I don't think we are separate from God, nor outside of God, or that God is out there some place pushing us around. I believe that God (or whatever the source of this vast, marvellous universe is), is wishing to express, separated into myriads of intelligent creative sparks. I believe we are to God like the drop of ocean is to the whole ocean. I believe we have been given these marvellous minds to be creative, and we have prostituted, destroyed and forgotten our capacities. In this particular age we are coming back.

It was an inspiring interview, like all of those I'd conducted around the Western 'gurus' of reincarnation. The insights I had learnt from Hazel Denning and the other researchers into past lives confirmed many facts that I had heard from the lamas of the East. The details of the 'coming back' might differ slightly, but the fundamental principles struck me as being remarkably similar. Reduced to its fundamental principles, the Western findings confirmed exactly what Lama Yeshe and Lama Zopa had told me in that tent pitched on the side of the hill at Kopan: that life continues after death; that the shape of that life is sculpted by the acts and intentions laid down in previous lives; that the state in which we die is of vital importance; that we meet up with people with whom we have 'karmic' connections; that our painful experiences are ultimately of our own making; that there is no 'blame' and that we are, without doubt, the authors of our lives.

10

LAMA OSEL

And what of Lama Osel – the most famous Western tulku of all? The last time I had seen him was in 1988 on the steps of the Kopan gompa, as I was putting the finishing touches to my book about him and his previous incarnation as Lama Yeshe. He was then just three years old and had announced, quite clearly, that he was going somewhere where there were big mountains and cows, 'far, far away'. I didn't know what he meant. Nobody had any travel plans for him. Was it fantasy, some active imagination on Lama Osel's part? In fact, a few weeks later the Nepal government cancelled the visas of all foreigners living in Nepal and Lama Osel, born in Spain, had to leave in a hurry. He went to Dharamsala in north India, once a hill station of the British Raj and now the home of the fourteenth Dalai Lama, his government-in-exile and a thriving Tibetan refugee population. In terms of travel time in that sub-continent it was indeed very far away. With the mighty Himalayas as a backdrop, and many a cow passing by, Lama Osel had obviously had some premonition of his next home.

This was the remarkable child who in the first few years of his life had been recognized by the Dalai Lama and Lama Zopa Rinpoche as the reincarnation of Lama Thubten Yeshe. He had been scrutinized by the pundits of Tibetan Buddhism and put through the traditional tests meted out to would-be tulkus, and had passed everything with flying colours. At the age of two he had been enthroned with as much pomp and ceremony as a British monarch, and had taken his place as one of the most prominent and unusual spiritual leaders of our time. From then on the former Western students of Lama Yeshe, and an increasing number of interested 'outsiders', would observe the Spanish boy lama in minute detail, watching for signs of authenticity and waiting for slip-ups.

Lama Osel was, after all, being held up as the most prominent example of reincarnation in our midst. While the other Western tulkus were quietly getting on with their mission, Lama Osel, on the other hand, seemed to have an extra dimension to his purpose on earth. His was very much the public face of reincarnation, in the spotlight almost since birth. This he took to with inordinate ease. From the time he was a baby and his identity was revealed he had faced public and press, crowds and disciples with a grace and detachment that were, quite obviously, completely natural.

I pondered on the fact that Lama Yeshe had, without doubt, been one of the biggest and earliest transmitters of Tibetan Buddhism to the West. His unusual and remarkable skill at putting across the ancient wisdom of his religion in Western terms, together with his charismatic personality, had inspired a huge number of followers and eventually a worldwide organization. It followed, therefore, that his reincarnation would also be high-profile, gregarious, at ease with the public, and ready to make his message known on a wide scale.

Still, it seemed a heavy burden for one so young, and I sometimes worried that my book increased his fame. Was it right? I asked Lama Zopa Rinpoche. Was it good for him? And Lama Zopa had answered that it was all part of Lama Osel's purpose here on earth, this time round.

Somewhat reassured, I continued to keep track of the little lama as he darted about the globe visiting his former students and demonstrating by his very being how this extraordinary new phenomenon of the tulku was working in the Western world. The next time I saw Lama Osel was in Pomaia, a country town nestling in the Tuscan hills, where the Italian students of Lama Yeshe had founded a centre. The Istituto Lama Tzong Khapa was housed in a large and impressive villa, and in the summer of 1989 it was full of visitors listening to the teachings of Lama Zopa and waiting for Lama Osel to arrive.

A year had passed, and physically Lama Osel had changed. He had lost the baby plumpness which made his small figure strangely similar to the round shape of Lama Yeshe, and the leanness of boyhood had set in. He was growing up.

Life, too, was becoming more serious. Lama Osel had a job to do in this life – the job of transmitting the holy Buddha dharma to the West – and the training for that awesome task was stepping up. He had been set on his way in Dharamsala, when HH the Dalai Lama had taught him the first letters of the Tibetan alphabet. This act secured the great man as Lama Osel's root guru, for, according to Tibetan belief, the person who gives you the means to understand the precious dharma is the foundation of all your attainments. At that time Osel was also receiving daily teachings from Lama Zopa Rinpoche and from an extremely tall and handsome monk called Yangste Rinpoche who was hailed as the reincarnation of a former teacher of Lama Yeshe. Lama Osel was devoted to this gentle young man. All in all, the spiritual talent lining up to teach Lama Osel was impressive indeed.

Now he was four, and his maturity was pronounced. He was bilingual in Spanish and English and had daily Tibetan lessons both in the rudiments of scripture and language. Maria, his mother, along with some of her other children, had driven from Spain to Italy to see Lama Osel. Together we crept up to the room where he was receiving his daily lessons in Tibetan prayers from Basili Llorca, his attendant, and waited outside the open door. Lama Osel had his back to us and was clearly intent on his studies. We watched and listened as Basili recited the lines of the prayer that Lama Osel had to memorize. The child got so far, and then stuck. Patiently Basili repeated the lines. Again Lama Osel stopped at the same place. This happened several times – and then Lama Osel raised his fist and beat his head several times, saying in a voice of sheer determination, 'I must get this into my head.'

Maria and I looked at each other in surprise. Here was no coercion. Here was a very little boy totally determined to learn a difficult prayer in a foreign language. The diligence was coming from him. Over and over again he spoke the Tibetan words, trying to get the pronunciation right. He was neither bored nor frustrated – just patiently committed to mastering the task at hand. He turned round, saw his mother, grinned – and then instantly turned back to his studies. He might not have seen her for months, but the lesson took priority. His concentration, as always, was remarkable.

Maria commented that she was surprised to see her young son taking his studies so seriously. 'It is unusual to see a child of his age feel so much responsibility to learn,' she said. It was, in fact, very touching.

Watching Lama Osel being so assiduously tutored raised the same vital questions: if Lama Osel was the reincarnation of Lama Yeshe, why was he having to learn the prayers anew? Later I had the chance to put the matter to an extremely high reincarnated lama, Ribur Rinpoche, who had once been the abbot of fifteen monasteries in Tibet. Then the Chinese had imprisoned him for some fifteen years, during which time he had been tortured for months on end and had his hands tied behind him day and night. It was reported that even under such dire conditions he had remained serene throughout, and had even cheered up his fellow prisoners. He seemed as good a person as any to ask about the intricacies of the workings of the mind. 'If reincarnated lamas have developed their minds to such a high degree, why aren't they reborn possessing exactly the same qualities?' I enquired.

'The point is,' he told me, 'they don't come as enlightened beings. They come as ordinary beings, and so they have to rely on a teacher. It's the same for all of them, including the Dalai Lama. They have to train – they have to bring out their qualities. It's very important. The tulkus come back through the power of loving kindness, compassion and altruism, whereas ordinary beings are reborn through the power of karma. This means they come back exclusively for the means of living beings. Since they do come again they don't come as enlightened, because they have to show how a person should train.'

The ultimate test for Lama Osel, however, would be the benefit he would bring to others. After all, we had been told, that was the only reason why he had been born.

Certainly at this age he was already showing signs of exceptional kindness and caring. It had been there as a toddler, when he anointed my mosquito bites with ointment, when he worried about animals being killed for food. It hadn't diminished one jot. Shortly after arriving, Maria told him her brother was ill in hospital in Spain. The effect of this news on Lama Osel was electric. He stopped what he was doing, went over to Basili, pulled on his sleeve urgently and said he wanted to leave immediately! He needed to go to Valencia to see his uncle and say prayers for him. Basili had a difficult time persuading him it wasn't possible. Later I learned that Osel always wanted to go to people who were sick.

Over the next few days I watched Lama Osel's growing sense of his role in life. As a baby he had naturally, almost automatically, been a tiny lama; now he was becoming conscious of it. He was perpetually smiling at people and seemed to mean it. He would stop what he was doing to greet newcomers and give them a blessing. His arrivals and departures by car were accompanied by much waving – just like those of a well-groomed royal child. He graciously posed for pictures whenever it was demanded of him. He happily passed round tea and biscuits if he received visitors in his room. In fact he was just like Lama Yeshe – warm, hospitable, considerate, outgoing and communicative, reaching out to people whenever and wherever he could.

But the most interesting development from my perspective was his growing assumption of the role of leader. Whereas before he had been happy to play with people, or by himself, now he was organizing games and gathering the youngsters of the centre around him. They flocked to him naturally, drawn by his magnetism and his infectious sense of fun. He was indubitably 'the boss'. Was this to be his new generation of followers? One of my most graphic memories of this time was the sight of Lama Osel loading up a cart with small children and, with the help of the bigger ones pushing from behind, pulling his cartload around the grounds while he led them in Tibet's most famous mantra, 'Om Mane Padme Hung' – Homage to the Jewel in the Lotus – which they belted out at the top of their voices!

His spiritual precocity was still in evidence. One afternoon he got hold of the pendant of Chenrezig, the Buddha of Compassion that his mother was wearing. 'Take this off,' he commanded. 'It isn't blessed. Only the Buddhas can bless it,' he said as he put the pendant on his altar in front of all his Buddha statues. Who knows how he knew it hadn't been blessed?

The same precocity reappeared during the puja, the long, ritualized religious ceremony held to pay homage to Osel as the guru. As always, Osel was surprisingly at ease sitting on the throne for some three hours at a time, dressed in the regalia of a high lama and watching Lama Zopa Rinpoche out of the corner of his eye for the cues to play his damaru and bell. At intervals he grinned at some monks and winked at others (a newly learnt trick), mixing comedy with the spiritual like Lama Yeshe. He rocked back and forth on his cushion, moving to some inner felt rhythm while reciting the Tibetan prayers he had learnt. He tried hard to do all the complicated hand mudras, attempting to fulfil his role with a touching sincerity.

It was when the selected monks and nuns stood to offer him gifts of food and incense that I saw the profoundest transformation. His whole demeanour changed. An air of exquisite serenity came over him. The atmosphere in the room became charged with a tangible stillness as, with downcast eyes and an aura of curious ancient wisdom in a body so young, Lama Osel listened to the chanted requests by the standing monks and nuns to please live long and help all sentient beings. This was Italy in 1989, but for a few minutes it seemed as though we had 'intersected the timeless moment', as T. S. Eliot said.

Then it passed. The puja was over. Lama Osel yawned widely, stood up from the throne and with a clenched fist above his head made the victory salute to Pende, the American monk who had been teaching him about baseball culture. It was back to normal.

Later, looking through the photograph album, I got a glimpse of the very unusual life that Lama Osel had been leading in the past year. A world tour had taken up much of the twelve months. There he was sailing in Hong Kong, there in Los Angeles at the Kalackara Initiation given by HH the Dalai Lama, there at Disneyland being hugged by Mickey Mouse, there again in Hong Kong with his arms around a young Chinese boy, the reincarnation of one of his closest friends from his previous life – the warmth between the two young boys was unmistakable. There he was making small Buddha figures with Lama Zopa Rinpoche; there he was in France playing computer games with a monk; there he was in Madison, USA with his former teacher, Geshe Sopa; there he was in Holland imitating a person meditating; there he was in Germany . . . and so on. It was a sophisticated life, but one which his attendant Basili Lorca insisted was not making him spoilt.

'He can deal with the travelling easily, although the change in food sometimes upsets him,' said the Spanish monk who had become mother, father, friend and teacher of Lama Osel. 'He gets a lot of attention, but he is too kind and too intelligent to be spoilt by it.'

It was Basili who was with Osel more than any other person. Did he notice any further signs of Lama Osel being a reincarnated high lama, Lama Yeshe perhaps?

'It depends on the situation. Environment is very important to him. Lama Osel, perhaps more than other chilren, is very quick to pick up the atmosphere and learn from the way others are. When he is with boisterous children he becomes noisy. When he is with other rinpoches, such as Ling Rinpoche, the relationship can be very good.

'In Dharamsala, where he was surrounded by lamas and scholars, he was much more like a lama than a small child. He would do clever things and give answers that a child wouldn't give. Of course, tulkus never say clearly who they are,' he said.

'At one point in Dharamsala a very high and old rinpoche came to do a retreat. During that time Osel woke up one morning saying his name – actually chanting his name. He wanted to go and see him and take him a katag. He insisted. So off we went. Sitting before this holy man, he enquired if he could ask a question. The rinpoche said "Yes." "Can you see the minds of all sentient beings?" Lama Osel asked. The rinpoche was very surprised at such a question coming from a young child. "I wish very much that I could. I am trying to achieve that," he replied. Lama Osel then saw a picture of the Dalai Lama in the rinpoche's room and remarked that the Dalai Lama was his guru too.

'But actually it is in the small things that I see the greatest signs,' Basili Lorca continued. 'One night after I had washed him, washed his clothes, given him supper and put him to bed – the usual routine – he said, "Thank you, Basili, for all you do for me. Thank you. You are so kind." This is not the usual behaviour of a child,' he said.

Anyone who knew Lama Yeshe could recall his extraordinary ability to thank people. Visions flashed back of him coming into the Kopan meditation tent, beaming at us left and right, hands together and saying, 'Thank you, thank you, thank you so much.' Gratitude, I later discovered, is a hallmark of true spiritual realization. Lama Yeshe had it. He not only thanked people for the obvious things, but he would find gratitude in himself for the most obscure reasons like someone sunbathing, or a traffic cop handing him a speeding ticket! For a small child to be aware and appreciative of the kindness of others was indeed most unusual.

Not that he was always a paragon of virtue. His mischief level was as high as his spiritual one. Maria, Basili and I watched as he occasionally hit out at a child who wanted a toy he was playing with. He often wanted to win at games, and he could be extremely bossy at times too. It seemed normal enough.

'I have to keep strong discipline. He's strong-minded, and needs strong means of control,' said Basili.

The 'strong means of control' was spanking. Lama Osel frequently felt Basili's hand on his bottom. While many of us disliked the amount of physical punishment he received, Lama Osel had his own disconcerting way of dealing with it. He would often turn round to Basili and say, 'I am not my body', or 'Thank you, Basili, for beating me.'

When tackled about the correctness of hitting him, Basili was unrepentant. He had been told by Lama Zopa that this was the correct way to reprimand Lama Osel, the way that all Tibetan children were taught to distinguish right from wrong. It was the Spanish way, too. 'The Dalai Lama, Lama Zopa, Lama Yeshe, all the great lamas have been spanked. It's normal. The important thing is that it is not done with anger,' he said.

The other contentious issue surrounding Lama Osel was the fact that he was separated from his family. In Tibet it was an accepted part of their culture that tulkus, when found, would be taken back to their former monastery to continue teaching and guiding others as they had in their previous life. The child himself (for it was usually a 'he') was normally only too willing to return to his former home, in spite of protestations from some parents. For Westerners, however, the fact that a small child like Osel was living apart from his mother and father was disturbing.

Maria and Paco were unusual parents. As a mother Maria had always expressed an unconventional belief that children should not be crowded, but given 'space'. She was completely and sincerely unclinging. She loved her children, but she did not need them to fulfil her. In fact, although she had babies with ease, she had never actually wanted a family. They just came, aided by her innate dislike of contraception or anything 'unnatural'. Besides, both Paco and Maria were devoted followers of Lama Yeshe. Inspired by his message of universal love and wisdom, they had established on the highest mountain in southern Spain a retreat centre which was open to practitioners of all faiths. With their devotion to Lama Yeshe and their trust in Lama Zopa it had not been so difficult for them to place their special son in Lama Zopa's care.

They had travelled *en famille* to Nepal to be near Lama Osel when he was in Kopan, but had been forced to return to Spain when the Nepalese government suspended all foreigners' visas. It had been a year since Maria had last seen Lama Osel, and now, in Pomaia, I asked her how she had coped with the separation.

'I know that real love is not attachment, and I try to develop this feeling with regard to my son. I have to share him with everyone,' she said. 'To be with Lama [Osel] for two hours is real happiness for me. To be able to come here to Italy and be near Lama for a few days gives me incredible joy. If he were with me all the time it would be just as it is with all my other children. We get angry and frustrated with each other, we never really have quiet moments together. So, I like this position very much.

'Someone is taking care of him perfectly. He is happy, healthy, clean, kind to everyone. I am delighted.

'Besides, after one year of being away from him I realize that Lama can manage very well without us. Lama has a very wide emotional world. He is not like other children who only have their immediate family to interact with. Lama has Lama Zopa Rinpoche and a global family. He also has no time to fret. His life is completely full.'

If Maria was sanguine about being separated from her son, Paco was feeling the wrench strongly.

'Paco misses him more than I do. I can intellectualize the situation and accept it, but Paco is more emotional. It goes straight to his heart,' she admitted.

She was right about Lama Osel not missing them. As always, he had shown an uncanny nonchalance about being parted from his family to lead a monastic life. This had been particularly noticeable when he was around two or three, the years when you would expect a small child to be devastated to find himself without his family, especially his mother. On several occasions in Kathmandu I watched with fascination the way he reacted when, after spending time with them, it was time for him to leave. I never saw him hesitate to say goodbye and get in the car to drive away. In fact he seemed pleased to get away from the hubbub of that large family to return to the peace of the monastery. Now, in Italy, the same dispassionate love was there.

It was not that he had no feelings for his family. He played with his siblings happily and always paid particular attention to his younger brother Kunkyen (Maria and Paco had given all their children Tibetan names), bringing him fruit and drinks and generally behaving in a deferential manner towards him. Whenever I returned from Kopan after spending time at Maria and Paco's house, Lama Osel would ask: 'Did Kunkyen bless you?' It was rumoured that be too was a 'special child', although no official overtures had been made towards him.

A year later Lama Osel's fondness for Kunkyen had not changed. 'His first question is to ask how he is,' reported Maria. Kunkyen was now three and, according to Maria, very strong-willed. 'He speaks a lot. He's like an actor, very funny – he bends his ears, things like that.' Here was another child to watch, I thought . . .

I asked Maria what struck her about Lama Osel's development in the twelve months since she had last seen him.

'I notice that his mind is always positive. He seems to be able to transform any situation into a party,' she replied. And then she remarked on a quality that I too had noticed: that Lama Osel didn't seem to be touched by the strength of his emotions like most of us are. If he is unhappy or sad it lasts for a few seconds and then he is out of it. It is almost as though he is wearing a mask for our benefit – to be normal.

'He doesn't have the same concepts of suffering that we have,' said Maria. 'He is completely in the moment. He wakes up immediately. If you tell him to stop playing he says, "OK." If it's time to go to sleep he says, "OK." If it's time to go it's OK. He can change from one situation to another without any problem. This is very unusual.'

As for her son's identity, Maria is clear: 'I don't have any doubts that Lama Osel has the mind of Lama Yeshe, but it's still developing. I still think of Lama Yeshe when I think of my guru. Maybe when I receive real teachings from him I will consider him my guru. Right now, however, I still call him *cariño*!' she said.

Another year passed before I saw Lama Osel again. He had spent the intervening months more quietly in a Tibetan monastery in Switzerland called Tarpa Choeling, set up by the late Geshe Rabten. The high mountain air, the healthy food, and the peace and routine of monastic life had suited him well. But in August 1990 Lama Zopa was coming to Holland to teach at the Maitreya Institute, founded by the Dutch students of Lama Yeshe in the beautiful woodlands of Emst, and Lama Osel and Basili had travelled there to be with him.

Lama Osel had grown up considerably and was taking charge more than ever. I arrived as a puja was about to begin, and hurried to join in. This time Osel didn't wait for anybody's cues. He launched right in, reciting Tibetan prayers one after the other at an impressive rate. I looked at him afresh and noticed that, in some way, he now seemed to be Lama Zopa's equal. Thankfully, the sense of humour was still intact. At one point he got a fit of the giggles which he successfully controlled. He grinned, made faces and struck a mock meditation pose – which looked hilariously like Lama Zopa. He knew it, but interestingly didn't laugh himself.

The discipline and the concentration which had been visible a year earlier had developed. A glass of orange juice was put in front of him, but it was an hour before he took a sip. At the back of the large room a group of children had got bored with the ceremony and were playing. He made no move to join them, nor did he cast any envious glance towards them. Instead he blessed each of them as they came up to him at the end to offer him the white scarf.

At the end of the puja Lama Zopa Rinpoche made a speech.

As always, behind the quiet delivery was a potent message: 'Today we have offered a long life puja to Lama, who passed away in his old aspect and has returned as a guide in his new aspect. Although I have a little dharma knowledge I travel from one country to another around the world. But until Lama Tenzin Osel Rinpoche is ready to teach sentient beings in the West and in other places, I plan to continue like this,' he said.

'We invite highly qualified teachers to be guest teachers at our centres, and when they come we receive them and we accept their kindness in helping us. But we must never, never forget that this is Lama's incarnation. Lama who has returned to us in his new form. We must not forget the one who has created all these centres.

'There are so many sentient beings who have come into contact with the dharma that we should not let Lama, who has come back in a new form, be forgotten while we are so fortunate in meeting other qualified lamas.

'I think it is my responsibility to say these things because Lama brought me to the West so often in the past to create this organization for his Western students.'

It was, it seemed to me, not only a promise that Lama Osel would indeed be teaching one day, but a warning that in the interim we must not lose sight of who our ultimate teacher was. What Lama Zopa was doing was shoring up the edifice of the worldwide structure of centres that Lama Yeshe had initiated, making sure it stayed steady until Osel could take the helm. Looking at the young boy sitting next to Lama Zopa, charmingly putting his hand up to his ear as if sneaking to catch words he was not supposed to hear, it sounded a dizzying plan. Osel was still five years old. So many things could happen.

I received a potent reminder of the Buddhist law that nothing stays the same when I met Maria again. Life might have been running smoothly for Osel in the past year, but she had been dealt a severe blow. Maria had discovered a large tumour in one of her kidneys. She told me the precise measurements: 8cm × 7cm × 6cm. It sounded enormous. The doctor advised her to have it out immediately. But, with her typical dislike for medical interference already evidenced by her attitude towards contraception, Maria had decided to wait before making her decision. In the meantime, with her usual sublime ease, she had produced another child, her seventh. She had also started up a tourist business in her home town of Bubion, to cater for the growing number of visitors who were beginning to discover the lovely little town.

Lama Zopa had then visited Spain, and she went to meet him to tell him of her sickness and seek his advice. 'If the guru said I should have an operation then I would have, even though I don't like doctors or hospitals. But Lama Zopa told me that this sickness was full of blessings for me. "It will help you practise. Now is the time to do a retreat – to control the illness," he said.' His words struck home, and for the first time in her life Maria was planning to plunge herself into serious meditation.

In fact the whole year had been difficult for Maria. The previous Christmas Eve she had had a car accident. She had been driving Lama Osel and Basili back to Bubion from Madrid when a car veered out of a side street in Granada and hit them. The driver had been celebrating for a good few hours. Maria had been jerked into the steering wheel; Basili had lurched forward and hurt his knee; and Lama, who had been sleeping in the back, fell to the floor, not hurt at all. Nevertheless they decided to go to the hospital to be given a check-up.

What happened there was extraordinary. The four-year-old Lama Osel took control. He had approached the doctor and said: 'Please take care of my mother, who has a pain in her side, and Basili, who has hurt his knee. I have nothing wrong, but you need to check them.' The doctor was rather nonplussed about being given orders by such a small patient and replied that he should be examined himself. 'No, there is no need. But please look after my mother and Basili,' he insisted.

A little later the doctor heard a knock on the door of the room where he was looking at X-rays of Maria and Basili. Osel walked in. 'Please can I enter, because I am very interested in this sort of thing,' he announced. The doctor took a second look, then recognized the child whose face was well known all over Spain. Suddenly this unusual behaviour became clear to him.

Lama Osel was also still capable of surprising even those closest to him with sudden 'revelations'. One day when he was in Switzerland his father Paco, an Italian monk and Basili took him to lunch at a restaurant with a balcony overlooking a valley. Lama Osel sat watching some birds flying down to the balcony looking for scraps to eat. Amid the general conversation Osel began to speak in a tone that made them all stop and listen. 'Before,' he said, 'many, many Buddhas came into my body, then I became tiny and entered into my mother's womb. Then I came out.' He paused, then added, "Before, I was Lama Yeshe. Now I am Lama Osel.'

The others were speechless. The birds flocking down to the balcony had obviously triggered off a memory of something that had happened before he was born. Nobody could be sure what exactly he was talking about, but all those present knew that when he was dying Lama Yeshe had performed his profound meditation where he would have visualized the Buddha Heruka, his personal practice, dissolving into him several times. According to the esoteric guidelines of tantric Buddhism, mastery of this highly complex meditation is essential in order for the spiritual adept to dictate the precise conditions of his next rebirth. Was this the many Buddhas dissolving into his body Lama Osel was talking about?

His statement about being Lama Yeshe before and Lama Osel now was one I had heard earlier in Kathmandu when he was only three. He had been playing with his brother Kunkyen and I had asked him outright if he was the reincarnation of Lama Yeshe. 'I am Tenzin Osel, a monk,' he had replied with great solemnity. 'Before, I was Lama Yeshe. Now I am Tenzin Osel.' I had marvelled then that at such a young age he had managed to find the words to express the complicated process of reincarnation. The continuity of the two beings was present, but the identification of the two personalities was different. I marvelled again now, when I heard the remarkable words that Osel had uttered after looking at the birds.

A few months later I saw him when he stopped over in London *en route* for the next stage of his extraordinary life. He was on his way to southern India to Sera monastery to begin his formal Tibetan education. He slipped his hand in mine as I showed him some of the sights. The swarming pigeons at Trafalgar Square did not impress him at all, but the creepy-crawly exhibition at the Natural History Museum did. He was engrossed by the minutiae of the insect kingdom, and would have stayed looking at the exhibits for hours had we allowed him.

He had duties to perform as well. He hosted a children's hot-chocolate party at the Jamyang Centre, in Finsbury Park, where he sat rapt in front of a video of *The Snowman*, twice. Although he had come down with a heavy cold he thanked the photographers for 'taking the trouble to come' and he willingly presided over a puja, although he must have been feeling awful. It was on this occasion that I noticed for the first time how adults, especially newcomers, often projected their own childhood experiences on to Osel.

One woman I spoke to said it was cruel to subject a small child to such a lengthy 'ordeal' when he should be tucked up in bed. She had been sent to boarding school at five and had been traumatized in the process. Another man commented that he thought Lama Osel looked bored by the whole procedure – and then added that he had spent much of his childhood in a similar state. Yet another woman didn't understand a word of what was going on but went away feeling inexplicably happy. As it was impossible that Osel was incorporating all these varying conditions I began to wonder if he was acting as a mirror, reflecting back to the observer states of minds and emotions that they possessed. If so, then he was truly fulfilling the role of the guru – for the real guru, the worthy, honourable guru, functions to reveal the disciple's own inner nature and thus to show what must be confronted, worked on or acknowledged.

For several happy hours I watched him at play: it was a fascinating spectacle. Someone had given him a model aeroplane designed for a seven-year-old. He sat down by himself to assemble the pieces, following the instructions and diagrams. When he reached a certain point he got stuck. Much to my surprise, he did not throw a tantrum or get frustrated as most children of five would have done; instead he calmly undid all that he had done and started from the beginning again. His concentration was immense and unusual. I recalled that concentration comes from hours of meditation. The ability to focus for hours at a time on a single task is the territory of the yogi. Could what I was witnessing be the result of Lama Yeshe's past efforts? Osel got to the same point in his plane-building, and again he could go no further. Again he took the model apart. Twice he built the aeroplane, and twice he disassembled it. On his third attempt he finally gave up, defeated by the difficulty of completing the exercise. He thrust it into Basili's hands. 'You do it!' he commanded.

Later I overheard someone talking to him. 'What do you want to do when you grow up?' they asked.

'Give teachings,' came the immediate reply. Then he added, seriously, 'But not now. Later.'

Did he know the Dalai Lama, and if so what did he think of him, they enquired.

'He is my guru,' said Osel almost dismissively, as though this was so obvious that it was hardly worth asking.

Later, he got up and led me by the hand upstairs to show me a photograph of Lama Yeshe hanging on the wall. 'That's me, before,' he stated in a matter-of-fact way. 'Then I got sick.' He did a mime of someone getting weaker and weaker and sagging. 'Then I died and they put me in a stupa and set fire to it,' he said, tongue lolling out. 'And now I am here,' he added cheerily. It was impressive. But at this age one could not be sure how much he had been told and what he intuitively knew. From now on, I thought, demonstrations of past-life recall would never be as thoroughly convincing as those he had given when he was a baby.

I saw him again over Christmas at Varanassi, also known as Benares, that ancient crumbling Indian city on the banks of the Ganges. I was on my way to Australia, Lama Osel was on his way to Sera monastery, and a vast crowd of 150,000 Tibetans were on their way to attend the Kalachakra Initiation to be given by the Dalai Lama at Sarnath, the place where the Buddha delivered his first teaching after reaching Enlightenment. The Kalachakra Initiation was one of Tibet's most esoteric and difficult practices, in which the Initiator would harmonize the inner elements of the body and mind to bring about harmony and peace in the outer world. The Dalai Lama had been performing this ceremony across the world in an attempt to stop humankind's destructive tendencies. Now it was Lama Osel's little figure which strode confidently on to the stage in front of that vast throng to present the representative offering to the great man.

Later he dressed up as Father Christmas to give presents to people in his hotel, and he ordered hot milk from a stall to be sent to the stray dogs milling around outside. On a more official note, he hosted a lunch party for all the young reincarnated high lamas who had come to the Kalachakra. It was an impressive gathering. They were all there; Ling Rinpoche (previous senior tutor to the Dalai Lama); Trijang Rinpoche (previous junior tutor); Song Rinpoche, who had been very close to Lama Yeshe and presided at his funeral; Serkong Dorje Change; and Serkong Rinpoche, the marvellous lama whose furrowed face and large, pointy ears had supposedly been the model for Yoda in the film *Star Wars*.

Curiously, their 'predecessors' had all passed away around the same time. It was said that they had chosen 'to die' in order to remove serious obstacles that were threatening the Dalai Lama's life. They had been the cream of the Gelugpa hierarchy, the lineage holders, all of them towering masters of meditation and scholarship. They had all been reborn around the same time as well. Now their reincarnations were assembled on the lawn of this smart Indian hotel.

'That's the entire future of the dharma,' remarked one perceptive onlooker. Lama Osel was among them, only his white skin and Western features setting him apart. Would they accept him, and vice versa, so easily when they were all old enough to realize the difference?

Maria too had arrived – to do her retreat in Bodhgaya. She looked well, but told me that apart from the tumour on her kidney she now had a secondary tumour on her brain. As she had refused surgery and medication the doctors had given her only six months to live, but this had not upset her at all. She was putting all her faith in the spiritual practices on which she was about to embark. Lama Zopa had told her to offer up her sickness, to use her tumours as a vehicle for taking on the sufferings of others.

This advice immediately took my mind back to Medjugorye, the small town in former Yugoslavia where the Virgin Mary has been appearing to six young people daily for a number of years. Fascinated by this phenomenon, I had gone there in my capacity as a tourist to see the site for myself. I had interviewed the visionaries, one of whom, Vicka, a vivacious girl of twenty-four, told me about the brain tumour she had developed. For months on end she felt sick and was continually fainting, but she kept up her cheerful disposition, insisting on talking to the pilgrims who came to hear her message.

She had told me that the Virgin Mary, or Gospa as she was called in Medjugorye, had asked her to offer up her brain tumour for the sickness of the world, and that it would be cured on a specific date. Vicka had duly written down the date of her promised cure, sealed it in an envelope and given it to the local priest for safe keeping. In the meantime she had refused offers of free treatment from a Harley Street specialist in London.

Her faith was rewarded. On the exact date that she had written down, the tumour suddenly vanished. Today Vicka radiates good health, and that inner joy which is invariably the signature of true spiritual experience. I wondered how Maria, the mother of Osel and six other children, would fare.

During the time we were at Varanassi we had our own teaching on death and impermanence. Lama Zopa's mother passed away literally in our midst. It affected us all deeply – especially Maria, the mother of the other famous lama.

We had all come to respect the tiny, frail, almost blind old lady known as Amala, who had insisted on making the long, arduous journey from her home near Mount Everest to the hot, dusty plains of India to see the Dalai Lama and receive the Kalachakra Inititiation. 'She is sleeping in a corner of a roof – crowded in with all the Kopan boys. Although she is the mother of Lama Zopa, she refuses to have a separate room. She says she is no one special. It made me very humble,' commented Maria.

On the last day of the Initiation, Amala had received personal blessings from His Holiness the Dalai Lama. At 10 p.m. that evening, at the conclusion of the Kalachakra, she passed away, her face illuminated by serenity and peace. She had received what she had come all this way for and had died saying the mantra that she had uttered millions of times throughout her life: 'Om Mani Padme Hum', the sacred words of Chenrezig, the Buddha of Compassion.

It was a mark of Lama Zopa's love for his students that he turned what could have been an occasion of private grief and recollection into a public event: he allowed us into the small room where his mother's body lay in the sleeping bag in which she had died, buried under piles of white scarves given in respect by the visitors. In spite of my apprehension at seeing a dead body, I was surprised to find the room filled with a sweetness, a delicacy and a tangible aura of something very vital, yet at the same time peaceful, going on. It remained like that for three days, when suddenly the expression on her face changed and with it the atmosphere in the room. At this point Lama Zopa Rinpoche announced that Amala had finished her meditation and had 'succeeded' in her death. It seemed a curious choice of words. In that singular phrase Lama Zopa had succinctly summed up the Tibetan Buddhist view that the death process was very much an individual challenge which could be controlled if we had the mind to do it.

The next day we were all invited to witness Amala's cremation at the ghats on the banks of the holy river Ganges. It was a rare opportunity to contemplate the meaning of Death and Impermanence. The body, placed upright and covered with piles of wood scented with incense and adorned with flowers, took two hours to burn. A friend asked a nearby monk if she could take a photograph. 'Yes – and use it as a meditation every time you feel depressed. It will put everything into perspective,' he replied.

Silently I thanked Amala for giving us Lama Zopa Rinpoche, the small, saintly man who had worked so hard and given so much to us Westerners. As I looked at the smoke swirling over the sacred river and the queue of corpses lined up along its banks waiting to be burnt, I thought how short and ephemeral this life was.

There was, however, no end to mind. It continues in an ever-flowing, ever-changing stream, like the great Ganges itself. To press home this most fundamental of Buddhist teachings even further, in case we had not got the point, a few years later we were to be presented with a young boy with an exceptionally intelligent face. He was sitting at Lama Zopa's feet in monk's clothes. He was, we were told, the reincarnation of Amala.

On 15 July 1991 Lama Osel Rinpoche, the reincarnation of Lama Thubten Yeshe, formally entered Sera monastery. He was six years old. As his small motorcade approached its destination, a red line could be seen in the distance. As the cars drew closer their occupants saw that it was the entire assembly of monks, who had turned out to line the road to welcome their newest incumbent. It was an honour accorded only to the highest lamas – but, it was agreed, Lama Yeshe certainly qualified due to his immense work in spreading the holy Buddha dharma across the world, and because of the prestige he brought to his monastery. To the monks of Sera, the small Western boy clasping his hands together and bowing in greeting had simply 'come home'.

Sera was awesome place and as far away as you could get from the archetypal image of a mysterious building clinging to a mountain peak. It was as big as a town, with streets, houses, dormitories, temples, kitchens, shops and dogs: a bustling, throbbing place pulsating with the vibrant, all-male energy of vast numbers of Tibetan monks. By the time Lama Osel arrived there were over two thousand of them, and their numbers were growing yearly as more and more fled from Tibet to seek the spiritual training that was denied them in their homeland. Lama Osel had entered the largest monastery in the world.

Sera was one of the three great monastic universities that the Tibetan refugees had painstakingly rebuilt in exile. It was of vital importance. Their monastic universities were not only the womb of their greatest spiritual, philosophical and meditational masters, they were also the bedrock of Tibetan culture.

Back in Tibet it was to the original Sera monastery, on the outskirts of Lhasa, that the young Thubten Yeshe had gone when he was just seven years old. There he began his austere, highly disciplined training which would lead eventually to a worldwide mission. It was a mighty place, founded in 1419 by Jamchen Choje Sakya Yeshe, a disciple of the famous Lama Tsong Khapa, the great reformer of Tibetan Buddhism and founder of the Yellow Hat sect. Ironically, in the light of the Chinese destruction that was to follow centuries later, Jamchen Choje Sakya Yeshe was twice sent to China to teach the Buddhist doctrine to the Emperor. By 1959, when the Chinese invaded, Sera monastery held a huge population of ten thousand monks. Although a quarter of these managed to escape to northern India, among them Lama Yeshe, many died from the unaccustomed heat and diet in the refugee camps.

Those who remained were eventually given a heavily wooded area in Karnataka state in southern India, about a two-hour drive west of Mysore. They set about clearing the space and building again the seat of learning that was to preserve their spiritual heritage and maintain the strength of their spiritual lineages.

Now, after Lama Osel's arrival, the ceremonies and welcoming parties went on for three days as the monastery officially offered him a place in their august place of learning, and in return Lama Osel offered them the traditional gifts of ceremonial pujas, food, money and tea, as well as a new well and substantial contributions to the Sera Health Project. It did not come cheap. The estimated cost of Lama Osel starting his new education was around US$50,000.

Lama Osel appeared happy in his new house, built specially for him in a quiet place on the outskirts of the monastery. It had a garden and a dog called Om Mani. On the morning after his arrival the abbot arrived at Lama's new house to greet him personally. Lama commented that he thought everything had gone extremely well. 'I dreamed before coming that first there was a lot of light coming up and I was down, then much light came down and I was up high,' he said. It was an auspicious dream.

Many Western students had arrived at Sera to witness this turning-point in Lama Osel's life. Among them were his parents, Maria and Paco. At one point during the investiture Maria and Paco stood up and walked out of the temple together – a symbolic gesture which formalized their willingness to give their child to the religious life. Although Osel had in fact been happily leading an independent life for four years now, as his parents physically turned their backs on him and walked away he looked a little wistful.

Now the serious work – the hours of study and the tough discipline – was about to begin in earnest. Lama Osel was being plunged into an extraordinary system – rich, wonderful and unique. Only Sera had the means to lay the foundation of the work that Lama Osel was destined to carry out. For only the Tibetan teaching system had the 'technology' for understanding the mind in all its manifold and subtle details.

The expectation was that Osel would become a holder of the lineage of teachings and initiations, which was possible only by passing through the special education of a Tibetan monastery and specifically the tulku training system. More significantly, it was felt that only an education in Sera could furnish Lama Osel with the credibility regarded as absolutely necessary for his future life as a teacher. No matter how inherently gifted as a spiritual master he might be, without the thorough training and qualifications available from Sera his work would be undermined.

For all this I, and many others, quaked a little at this next phase in Osel's life. He was after all, a Western child with a Western mind, and Sera was – well, so *Tibetan*. It was also steeped in the framework of a six hundred-year-old tradition which had not changed much over the years. Many of us wondered how Lama Osel, with his love of computers and Michael Jackson music, would fare within the rules and rigid protocol of this strong Tibetan experience.

Maria voiced the concerns that a few of us were feeling: 'Lama's temperament is free, creative and spontaneous. He learns by reason. If you explain things to him he grasps it very quickly. In the traditional Tibetan system, however, learning is done by rote. They learn all the prayers, all the scriptures, by heart – and then when that is accomplished they debate on the meaning. This is not the Western approach to education, and in my view is rather archaic.'

Osel's day was now broken into strict periods of learning: 7 a.m. get up; prayers before breakfast at 8 a.m.; Tibetan language class from 9 a.m. for two hours; then Spanish class for one hour; lunch at noon; 1 p.m. – 3 p.m. English reading, writing and maths; 5.30 p.m. lessons with his Tibetan teacher; dinner; bed at 9 p.m.

It was indeed a tough regime, with the emphasis for the first few years on memorization and getting used to the monastic discipline. He was aiming eventually for a geshe degree, equivalent to a doctor of divinity, which back in Tibet took some thirty years to achieve. Here in Sera the process had been speeded up, but still there would be years of rigorous learning and debating before Osel was through. I wondered if he would stick it out.

I thought back to Lama Yeshe, and the way he had broken with the traditional methods of teaching to reach us Westerners. He had once told me he didn't care, that he was prepared to use *any* technique to get his audience to understand the Buddha dharma. That was his great appeal – his ability to communicate the way of the Buddha with his whole body, with gestures, with antics, with his marvellous sense of humour and with his spontaneous acts of kindness and love. He was not a conventional lama at all, on the outside at least. He knew that Westerners were not interested in the strict Tibetan presentation of the dharma and so had found his own highly individualistic way of teaching it. Part of me baulked at the idea of Lama Osel returning to the system which Lama Yeshe had, in the outer form, moved away from.

Still, Lama Zopa had decreed quite unequivocally that it was best for Lama Osel to go to Sera. And who were we to dispute that great man, who cherished Lama Osel more than his own life? He had taken enormous care in choosing Lama Osel's gen-la, the Tibetan geshe who was to teach the boy the Tibetan language, the memorization of texts and Lam Rim (the step-by-step guide to Enlightenment) subjects. He was a gentle, kind man and one of the best teachers in Sera. As Lama Zopa pointed out, the conditions provided for Lama Osel were all-important. So, for all its possible drawbacks, Sera had incomparable benefits to offer. We could only wait and see the outcome.

Not that Lama Osel's Western roots were being totally forgotten. In order to help build a bridge between the two ways of life Lama Zopa, with his infinite care, had arranged for a Western tutor to be brought into Sera to furnish Lama Osel with the beginnings of a Western education alongside the traditional Tibetan Buddhist one. The advertisement placed in the top newspapers in London, New York and Australia revealed the enormity and extraordinary nature of the task:

PRIVATE TUTOR – to provide full primary education to highest international standards for six-year-old Spanish reincarnation of former Tibetan Lama Thubten Yeshe. Tuition to run in parallel with a traditional Tibetan monastic education to be provided by others. Tuition to assist the young Lama to integrate Western and Eastern curricula in preparation for a life of teaching.

Primary instruction medium English, secondary Spanish. Location South India eight months, Europe one month per year. This unusual and challenging assignment requires a person of highest integrity, five to ten years' tutoring experience and impeccable references.

The person who won the job from hundreds of applicants was Norma Quesada-Wolf, a classicist in her early thirties from Yale University. Born in Venezuela of an American mother and Spanish father, and with ten years of Zen Buddhist meditation behind her, Norma seemed tailor-made for the job. With her husband John she moved into Sera armed with an independent study programme from the Calvert School in America, which not only set out a tutoring schedule for Lama Osel but provided means for independently assessing his progress as well.

Peter Kedge, a board member of the FPMT (Foundation for the Preservation of the Mahayana Tradition) and long-time student of Lama Yeshe, had conducted the search for the right tutor. He explained the hopes for Lama Osel's education: 'Great emphasis is being placed on providing Lama Osel with a strong basic Western contemporary education so that, in his later years, the "language" he uses to explain molecular physics will be the same as when explaining emptiness – the aim being to cross the boundaries of the Eastern mind and the Western mind, exposing their similarities.' It was a mighty plan indeed, but one could not help but be a little apprehensive at the load of expectations and aspirations that was being put on a pair of small, six-year-old shoulders.

The observations of Norma Quesada-Wolf, as a newcomer to this extraordinary scene of Western reincarnate lamas, were particularly interesting. Her first impression was of a child who played hide-and-seek, then showed her and her husband the Buddhas in his room, the watercolours and drawings he had done, and where a certain lizard lived. He then asked if they were tired from their journey, turned to someone and asked, with natural dignity, if they had been offered tea.

'I suppose I was expecting to find a wise, very serious little figure, someone like Teddy in the J. D. Salinger story of the same name. But while Lama certainly does have this aspect, I had not anticipated how light-hearted and charming he would be,' she said.

With professional interest she also noted what many amateur observers had seen on many occasions – Lama Osel's unusual powers of concentration and his ability to be totally absorbed in what he was doing.

'There's something special about him. He has a capacity for concentration, for remembering, and for invention and imagination that seems to me to be beyond the capacities of an average child. When something holds his interest, whether it be playing with Lego blocks or doing a lesson, he just disappears into it and remains in that thing for long stretches of time, constantly thinking about it, imagining it, playing with it, and seeing it from all different perspectives.'

Her words immediately flashed me back to another time when Lama Yeshe was talking about how we perceived things. He took as his example a flower. Never has a flower been looked at in the depth in which Lama Yeshe saw it. He examined all its parts, he considered its perfume and its effect on our sense of smell and an insect's, he talked about its aesthetic properties and how the flower had been an object of poetry, intuition, love and admiration, and how this differed from culture to culture. Through this intense and detailed scrutiny Lama Yeshe was trying to get us to see the totality of things through varied levels of meaning.

In fact Lama Yeshe had very clear views about how children

should be educated. Using his graphic, idiosyncratic style of English he delineated his beliefs in a system which he called 'Universal Education':

A narrow presentation of the world in education suffocates children. It brings frustration and blockage that interrupts the child's openness to learning. Children do not want to be trapped by limitations. If one shows them the reality of things which is beyond all limitations, their enthusiasm for learning will never cease and the individual will become a totally integrated person.

Any explanation is incomplete if there is no logical reference, no intellectual basis for it. Behind this base there must be a psychological explanation and a philosophical framework. Then the totality in all its aspects becomes so profound, so profound. In other words, contained in an entire subject are the essence of religion, philosophy and psychology without any separation, existing simultaneously. In this way the person becomes integrated. In the world today these have become separated. Really, you cannot separate them.

We cannot make divisions such as: you are the spiritual person, you are the philosopher and you are the psychologist. All of reality is contained, potentially and now existent, in everybody. Education should be everything to come together, not separating, not partial.

The bad in the world, in my opinion, is religion separated from life, from science, and science separated from religion. These should go together . . .

It was a system that was now tallying with Lama Osel's own approach to learning.

Certainly Osel was enraptured by science in the form of anything to do with outer space, and had numerous books on space and space travel which he discussed in detail with Norma. She noted, however, that he would often put his comic book stories of Superman and Batman into a dharma context, working out the morals of the 'goodies' and 'baddies' according to Buddhist belief.

He also showed an aptitude for mathematics and was fascinated by large numbers, vast distances, huge sizes and great weights – in fact, anything big. In the past few years he had also become fascinated by illusion and magic, and would often play games where he pretended to make things appear and disappear. He was also genuinely enthralled by the minutiae of the insect kingdom, as I had seen in London's Natural History Museum, and in the evolution of species. Osel's was a broad mind – just like Lama Yeshe's.

Norma noted other character traits, too – Lama's equally famous strong-mindness, and the fact that he often wasn't a 'model' child. 'When something doesn't interest him, it is impressive how he can invent one way after another, non-stop, to divert his and your attention from the thing at hand. He has a strong will and high spirits, and is very independent-minded.'

This again was reassuring. Norma was verifying what many of us had witnessed – that Lama Osel was not in any way a malleable person. He was very much his own person. It was gratifying, for one of my greatest concerns was that Lama Osel would be 'conditioned' into his present role, thereby detracting from the authenticity of his identity. How much more satisfactory to have a lama who was full of life and mischief and who could think for himself.

As she looked at the child who was now under her care, Norma saw further signs that Osel was out of the ordinary. On one occasion during an English lesson she was asking him for the opposite meaning of words. She would say 'up' and he would reply 'down', for instance. When she asked him for the opposite of 'asleep', however, he replied 'Buddha!' It was an astute and subtle answer, and a remarkable one for a child of his age. Not many adults are aware that the definition of a Buddha is a fully awakened being. Later she was to describe Lama Osel as a 'brilliantly gifted child'.

Educationally, in fact, Lama Osel was doing well across the

board. His gen-la, Geshe Gendun Chopel, announced that his charge was exceptionally intelligent and, even though he too noticed the boy's fondness for play, he felt that it would abate naturally as he grew older and understood the importance of studying. He also remarked that, although at first he had regarded Lama Osel as an ordinary child with the status of a tulku, since getting to know him he now considered him to be extraordinary, with an exceptionally clear memory.

But in spite of his excellent school reports, like many a small boy Osel often complained at having to study and told visitors he was 'too busy'. Once he was overheard saying: 'Don't you know I learn when I am playing?' He was, of course, absolutely right.

For a while, in the change-over period between Kopan and Sera, a warm and funny Australian monk called Namgyal was co-attendant of Lama Osel along with Basili Lorca. Namgyal's more artistic, less conventional personality found a link with those same aspects in Lama Osel's nature, and the two soon formed a strong bond.

'We used to sneak out together to eat pizzas, and we used to cook together,' he reminisced to me one day in Dharamsala, where I had gone to interview the Dalai Lama. 'Lama Osel, like Lama Yeshe, adores cooking. I gave him an apron which read "Never Trust a Skinny Cook", which he loved. We used to roll out dough together to make these pizzas and he would say things like "The cheese isn't correct." He is such a perfectionist! Everything has to be just so. He always wanted everything to be clean and proper. I remember him telling off the Tibetan lamas for slurping their soup, and they would laugh and laugh!'

Namgyal's encouragement of self-expression showed results in Osel's spiritual practices too. 'Every day we'd fill the water bowls with water, representing the offerings of flowers, light, music, incense and so forth to the Buddhas. Lama Osel loved it. He'd invent different ways to make these offerings. He'd put the little crystal bowls in various different patterns and add colouring to the water. It took much longer, but he showed me what creativity could do to transform a fairly mechanistic daily rite.'

This was so like Lama Yeshe, who would transgress the conventional monastic rule by creating his own altars – full of diverse, imaginative objects like shells and clay animals that represented things that were precious to him. Once he put a toy aeroplane on his altar, as that was the hallowed means by which he could reach sentient beings around the globe. And, having come out of Tibet and discovered such luxurious aromas as Patou's 'Joy' perfume, he quickly discarded the usual sticks of incense for the most expensive scent that money could buy. Only the best was good enough for the Buddha.

Lama Osel was following suit. His prayers and meditations under Namgyal's guidance were also taking a more individual-istic and creative turn. One day, after offering up the mandala to all the Buddhas, Lama Osel turned to him and said: 'Do you know what I visualized?'

'No,' replied Namgyal.

'I visualized Buddha in the sky and this mountain of ice cream and sweets and all different-coloured beautiful flowers all coming to the Buddha and entering into him.'

It was a perfect offering from a small boy.

'I asked him once if he missed his family,' Namgyal told me. 'He replied, quite seriously: "Lamas don't have families."'

For all the fun they had together, Osel also showed his Australian friend some of his special qualities. 'He has psychic abilities. One night he woke up and said that some spirits were trying to push over his altar. I felt he was quite in tune with spirits, and so I accepted what he said. The next day he did a puja for them because he said they were suffering. He also told me that in my last life I was a lama in Kham, a province of Tibet. That was interesting, because it verified what I'd been told by a Tibetan oracle some time previously,' reported Namgyal.

Other monks confirmed that Lama Osel would from time to time see into not just their past but their future as well. One said that Lama Osel had looked him straight in the eye and told him, 'Again you are going to be a lama, and I will hold you in my arms.' At other times he would scare them witless by declaring they were going to the hell realms – whether these were true prophecies or false no one was in a position to judge.

As time went on Namgyal saw other unusual behaviour which made him feel that Lama Osel was different. 'Once, when we were in Kathmandu, Lama Osel saw a woman light up a cigarette. He turned to me and said, "Should I tell her that she is killing herself?" I stopped him, but when I reported the incident to Lama Zopa he said I should have let him because later, when Lama Osel is grown up and well known, she might think about what he told her and change.'

At another time he accompanied Lama Osel to Bodhgaya, the place where the Buddha achieved Enlightenment. Here they met Kunnu Lama Rinpoche, a famous spiritual master so revered that even the Dalai Lama has been seen to prostrate to him. Namgyal told me what happened: 'When they met, Lama was completely overwhelmed with devotion towards Kunnu Lama and wanted to offer him all his toys, his watch, his torch, in fact anything that he could put his hands on! Afterwards Lama Osel said that Kunnu Lama Rinpoche was a Buddha and that he would never lose the photograph that Kunnu Lama had given him.'

After his post as co-attendant came to an end, Namgyal missed the company of his unusual charge. The intimacy that Lama Osel was able to evoke was powerful and precious. 'For a while I became Lama Osel's best friend. He used to tell me everything. Every night he'd confess to me all the things he'd done wrong, and his secrets like how he wanted to see girls without clothes on. I just treated these things as completely normal. He was so loving, so spontaneously affectionate. He loves being close to people. He'd lean across the table in front of others and say, "Namgyal, I love you." I will never forget Lama's love – never,' he said.

Life was beginning to change at Sera, and so was Lama Osel. After Namgyal left, Basili did too on 'advice' from Lama Zopa. No one was sure why. Perhaps, I thought, it was to prevent any single person getting too attached to Lama Osel. Or maybe it was because a monk's ultimate task is to lead a life of prayer and meditation, rather than to be a child-minder. There followed a series of Western monks assigned to look after the daily needs of the young Spanish tulku.

Now Lama Osel was beginning to grow up and increasingly to develop his own personality. In one way it was as if the mantle of the Lama Yeshe persona was slipping away, receding into the past, to allow the new being, Lama Osel, to emerge. We all had to see that Lama Osel was a different entity from Lama Yeshe, albeit connected in essence. Not only was he now looking very different from his 'predecessor', with his fine face, slim body and long, thin fingers, but he was also dropping his amenable, instantly lovable, infinitely charming presentation to the world. He was becoming a powerful force to be reckoned with.

I thought it could not be an easy process sloughing off such a strong, magnetic character as Lama Yeshe's and the heavy cloak of projections that so many former students put on him. About this time I had a dream which might have been an indication of how Lama Osel was feeling. In it he was dressed in robes and walking along a path, his head bowed and with an air of consternation about him. He looked up and said: 'When I was younger I knew I was Buddha, but now I am not so sure.'

The lines of William Wordsworth's famous poem 'Intimations of Immortality', learnt at school, came to mind:

> But trailing clouds of glory do we come
> From God, who is our home:
> Heaven lies about us in our infancy!
> Shades of the prison house begin to close upon the
>   growing boy . . .

The sentiments weren't entirely Buddhist, but the message was remarkably similar.

Osel was now challenging nearly everyone with whom he came into contact – by a word, a look, a rebuke, a refusal to cooperate. No longer Mr Nice Guy, he was throwing people back on themselves. No one found it very comfortable. Everyone had to admit, however, that his mind was becoming increasingly sharp, his perceptions uncomfortably accurate and his power undeniably great. The stories that emerged from those who saw him at this time illustrate the point.

'Over the past year or so he has been incredibly wicked to me,' reported Robina Courtin, a much-loved and respected nun, instrumental in setting up the FPMT's publishing company Wisdom, who had known Lama Yeshe for ten years. 'Every time I've seen Lama Osel recently he's said something awful to me. And he's absolutely spot on, every time. I'm not trying to be romantic, but it's as though he is Lama Yeshe and he is teaching me. It started when he was about four and we were out to lunch and he said in front of everyone, 'You talk too fast, you eat too fast; you walk too fast, you do everything too fast.' He said it with complete clarity. He knew exactly what he was saying. In the past eighteen months I have learnt more about my own speedy, berserk nature and the harm it does to others from Lama Osel than I have in my whole life.

'I have always known it, but until now I have never paid deep attention to it. I walk into his room and already I'm nervous because I know that, like Lama Yeshe, he's always catching me out. He says, "Why are you nervous?" It sounds so silly, but I know that I listen to what he says, not like [I would to words from] an ordinary child. He calls me Ani Nervous. All I can tell you is that it doesn't make me angry, like it would with any other child. He has helped me see myself more clearly than any other person. It can be very painful at times,' she admitted.

As Robina talked, I could hear Lama Yeshe's voice saying quite clearly, 'Buddhism should *shake* you. It is not meant to be comfortable. It must shake you out of your deluded way of seeings things! Then it is good.' 'Holiness, it seemed, was not always sweet and comforting. No one who had ever seen Lama Yeshe shaking thieving porters by the neck, or delivering a crushing reprimand to a student, or even wielding a stick to a misbehaving monk at Kopan, could forget that terrifying sight. Lama Yeshe might well have been infused with an exquisite capacity for love, compassion, humour and kindness, but he could bare his teeth and brandish his spiritual sword in the air if he felt the occasion demanded it. And Robina remembered, too, that at times Lama Yeshe was very tough with her. 'When I see Lama Osel it's very clear to me that his behaviour is specific. I see him with other people and he's gentle, sweet, kind. It's a super-personal thing.'

And then there was the time at Sera when an Indian girl came to have lunch with Osel. She was lovely, with a long plait of beautiful hair and an expensive sari. Lama Osel just sat there, like Lama Yeshe, listening to everyone talk. Then he asked the woman her name and she replied it was Goddess from the Ocean. Osel remarked that she shouldn't have pride because she had such a name. The way he said it stopped everyone, including the woman, in their tracks. It wasn't said rudely, just straight. The truly remarkable fact about this episode was that the pride he had picked up was extremely subtle. It wasn't obvious in her at all – she appeared to be a very humble person.

Similarly, he had been outraged when he learned that a wealthy nun had lent money to build a stupa. 'What do you mean "lend"?' he had shouted at her. 'Why didn't you give? You are very naughty. I am going to spank you.'

There was another occasion when he reprimanded a woman for being rude. 'It was devastating, but true,' she said. 'I do come straight out with things. We had gone to dinner in Bangalore and the waiters were fussing around and I spoke sharply to them. Lama Osel observed this and was very nice to them. Later he told me off. The extraordinary thing was that he didn't say so at the time, but waited till we were alone. That was what was so unusual.' She added: 'On another occasion

I had been sharp with some little monks who I could see had only come to play with Lama because he had Western toys. Osel turned to me and said, "You are not very kind, are you?"'

There was no malice, no vindictiveness in these statements, just the need to point out people's faults and to guide them on to more constructive paths. This was illustrated well in Taiwan, where Lama Osel met a man with clairvoyant abilities who told him about the third eye. Lama paused and then asked, 'Do you use your third eye just to see things or to help people?' His remark went straight to the heart of the matter – for what else is spiritual prowess for if not to benefit other sentient beings?

In this rather fearsome way Lama Osel was demonstrating that he was becoming a teacher in the true Buddhist style: reading people's minds and pointing out their negative tendencies in order that they might transform them. Hadn't the Buddha's way been one of confronting reality and then doing something about it? In particular Osel was now wanting people to 'check up', to examine their motivation, their mindfulness. Even when he was being spanked he would look at the person and say, 'Are you angry, are you angry?', with no tone of personal fear but only to discover if the cardinal error of anger was present in the act. He was also constantly challenging people's beliefs, especially about reincarnation. It was unnerving, said Michael Lobsang Yeshe, a Western boy who had been brought up in Kopan under Lama Yeshe's strict eye and who found himself looking after Lama Osel. 'He managed to bring out everything within me, and when I was at the highest point of my rage he would make comments such as: "Do you really believe that I am Lama Yeshe's reincarnation?" What puzzles me is how he can be a very intelligent, wise and strong lama one moment, and just when I am about to feel "Oh, he's really great", the next moment he is a very clever, naughty child.'

But there was more than the emergence of a teacher – for the first time in his life Lama Osel was beginning to rebel. He started to play up at lessons, finding brilliant strategies to get out of working, and, perhaps more seriously, showing signs that he found religious ritual and practice less than interesting. He would go into fierce tantrums if he felt he was being 'forced', putting those in charge of him on the spot. Some put it down to having to obey too many rules and having too many expectations put upon him.

'It's hard for both of us when he has to be the perfect lama,' said Michael. 'I have to see him without any faults and behaving very well. And from his side, he has to put on this act of being a perfect, well-behaved lama. After all, he is a human being like every one of us, and I think we ought to give him his space and time. But also, because he is a human being we should be very careful not to spoil him with too much admiration. We all have the responsibility of bringing him to what we all want him to be: a world teacher,' he said.

Lama Osel's new outbursts of wilful behaviour put us into a dilemma. How should we respond? Should we reprimand, ignore or take notice? Was it a spoilt child who was saying these harsh, rude things? Or was it a wise guru? For the Tibetans this was not even an issue. Tulkus are renowned for their great energy, their mischief, their strong will and their utter determination to take the lead. They are notoriously naughty and wild, and so for their own good must be dealt with by a strong hand. The Tibetans had no qualms about disciplining their spiritual adepts, on the grounds that their extraordinary power must be channelled into useful directions.

We Westerners, however, were new to the job. This was the first Tibetan tulku to be born as one of us, and we were having to learn the hard way how to deal with such an extraordinary situation and with the enormous responsibility that it entailed.

In the summer of 1993 the crisis struck. For the first time in his short, incredibly rich life Lama Osel rebelled outright. Something was definitely wrong, but who knew precisely what? Certainly there had been some great upheavals in his life since he had entered Sera monastery. The problem could have been the departure of Basili, his close attendant for so many years, leaving Osel with a series of other monks, kindly but not nearly as expert in handling a Spanish tulku with high spirits and a demanding lifestyle. It could have been the harsh discipline of Sera monastery which went against his free spirit and his passion for play. It could have been that he was worried about his mother, who he knew had cancer. It could have been the sudden and sad break-up of his parents' relationship. Or it could have been that, as he matured, he could see the awesome task that lay ahead of him, the lifetime of service and devotion, and wanted out. Whatever the reason, he sent plaintive messages both to Lama Zopa and to his mother, saying that he wanted to leave.

Lama Zopa was deeply concerned but, remembering his own inclination to run away from his monastery when he was a young child, and his several attempts to do so, ignored the request. He sincerely felt that this was a normal boyhood reaction to serious study, and was utterly convinced that Lama Osel's path necessitated the strong foundation in Tibetan Buddhism which only Sera could provide. He, and so many thousands of other young lamas, had survived the rigours of monastic life and had subsequently been extremely grateful for them, and he was confident that Lama Osel would eventually feel the same. But still Osel's pleas touched his heart. After all, the happiness of his guru meant everything to him. He went into deep meditation to ponder the dilemma that had suddenly arisen, but always the answer was the same – Sera monastery was where Lama Osel should be at least until he was thirteen. Lama Zopa publicly stated that this year was to be a crucial one for Lama Osel. Now was the time when he would decide what he wanted to do. Lama Osel's life was finally his.

However, when Maria heard her son's cries, with the boldness which characterized the other facets of her life she promptly flew into Sera, gathered Osel up and, without further ado, swiftly took him back to Spain. To say that the abbot of Sera and the rest of the monks were flabbergasted would be an understatement. It was an unprecedented move, unheard of in Tibetan history, and one that would only be performed by a European woman of particularly strong character. To lose their famous tulku was a terrible blow which cut them all deeply. The dramatic departure also created considerable shockwaves among the Westerners who learned the news. What was going to happen now? What of the great scheme that had been envisaged for Lama Osel and his work in the future? Was he truly the reincarnation of Lama Yeshe, or had it all been a terrible mistake?

To settle some of these disturbing questions I once again made the journey to the little Andalusian town of Bubion. It was mid-July and the ghastly pall of pollution that hung over the Costa del Sol, shrouding the once beautiful landscape in a thick yellow smog, matched my mood of apprehension. My two previous visits to Bubion had been in autumn and winter. Then the leaves were turning into glorious colours, and later the road was so snow-bound that I had to abandon the car halfway. Now, as I left the coast and drove up the steep mountain road, I noted how different it all was in high summer. The ground was parched, a strong smell of pinewoods filled the air, and only the cicadas broke the heavy silence of the siesta.

Bubion itself was as charming as ever, with its whitewashed houses glinting in the sunshine, its tiny balconies cascading with red and pink geraniums, mauve and scarlet bougainvillea, and its tiny cobbled streets where cars can manoeuvre with only millimetres to spare on either side. In the six years since I had been there it had obviously become more fashionable, as buildings had gone up everywhere and there were more tourists roaming the lanes. But miraculously the local people still worked their fields with hoes and sickles, the goats and sheep still had bells tied under their chins (which still woke you up at 5 a.m.), and the town still echoed to the sound of ever-flowing water coursing down the many irrigation channels built centuries earlier by the Moors.

I booked into the main hotel, with its vine-covered restaurant overlooking Spain's highest mountains and the sheer
valleys beneath, and thought it wasn't such a bad choice as a
birthplace. Then I went in search of Maria and Osel.

I found him in the family house (extended now to cater
for the ever-growing numbers), playing with his younger
brothers. His hair was still very short, but he was wearing
shorts and a T-shirt – a somewhat startling sight after years
of seeing him in robes. His spirits were as high as ever as he
cajoled his brothers to sneak up on me, but his face looked
drawn and he had heavy rings under his eyes. He didn't seem
particularly happy. Maria appeared and we went to have a
coffee and talk about what had happened.

'For me it was very obvious that something was wrong,
and I couldn't sit back without anything being done,' she
explained. 'I went to Sera last year, in 1992, to check out
Lama's situation. I was delighted by some things I saw, but
disturbed by others. Even then he had a lot of anxiety, because
there were so many things he wanted to do, new things, and
yet he was restricted. The fears I had about the formal Tibetan
education were coming true. I felt that Lama was being
continually frustrated, that the tulku education system was
subduing Lama's will but not fulfilling Lama's personality.

'He was bored with the memorization process that Tibetan
Buddhism requires for the first few years. He wants to *understand* through reason and stimulation. More importantly, he
was beginning to reject wearing robes, saying prayers and
being a lama. I believe these were violent reactions to a
situation that was making him unhappy,' she continued.

'What shocked me most, however, was Lama's behaviour.
Because he was miserable and frustrated, he was developing
a tyrannical ego, wasn't able to share with others and was
becoming very self-centred. This, I think, is partly to do with
the tulku training centre, where they school the child to be the
centre of attention and apart from other children. But it is also
partly to do with Lama's Western disciples who have not been
taught how to treat him. So often they give and give – anything

he wants – just to win his love and approval. They give in order to get. It's not good for him. It's also made him confused and unhappy.'

The reason why she had brought him back to Spain was not, she assured me, because she had reversed her decision about giving her son to the lamas, and wanted him with her. 'I still do not feel any maternal attachment. I freely offered Lama to Lama Zopa Rinpoche, and the easiest thing for me would be to leave the situation as it was. But I was Lama's chosen mother, and for that reason feel I have some responsibility to provide him with the best possible conditions in which to continue Lama Yeshe's work,' she said.

For all the present upheaval, the irrepressible Maria's conviction that her son was the reincarnation of Lama Yeshe had not faltered. Nor had her belief that his destiny was to carry on Lama Yeshe's mission of bringing the sacred knowledge of Tibetan Buddhism to the West.

'Everything is Lama Yeshe's strategy. He discovered his own limitations when he began to teach Westerners, which is why in this life he took a Western body. It is wrong to expect Lama Osel to appear as Lama Yeshe. This is a new vehicle, a new time, new parents. The causes and conditions are different. I believe that what Osel does depends on the conditions we provide. If we sow nice seeds now, then we will get a nice plant in the future. I believe that even all these upheavals are Lama Yeshe's trajectory. He's moving structures, bringing about new orders,' she reasoned.

Sitting opposite me with her shining eyes, she looked remarkably well considering that two years earlier she had been given no more than six months' life expectation. In fact the secondary cancer in her head had disappeared completely, much to her doctor's astonishment. The tumour in her kidney was still there, but she had learnt to treat it like a friend, she said.

'It gives me no trouble at all. It has grown to follow the exact shape of the kidney but without obstructing any of the arteries, so it has not prevented the kidney from functioning.'

She was an extraordinary woman, bold, brave and with an independent spirit prepared to challenge all given beliefs.

In the meantime having Lama Osel in Bubion was, as she foresaw, not an easy option. She was still trying to maintain his special regimen as a tulku, keeping his living quarters separate from those of the other children, and attempting to make him do his daily prayers and practices. At the same time she was running her newly established tourist business for the area, and overseeing the welfare of her other children. Even for Maria this workload was enormous. Now, in July, the children were on holiday and Lama Osel, freed from the restrictions of Sera, was running wild. To make matters worse, after their separation Paco had left Bubion to work in London. He was absolutely against what Maria had done and fervently believed that Lama Osel's problem was primarily one of resisting getting down to hard work.

To resolve the situation, Maria had come up with a plan to start her own school for tulkus in Bubion. It was audacious, to say the least. She had it all worked out. 'It will be a unique environment for special children, Tibetan and Western alike, who will be trained to meet the demands of our rapidly changing world. I would like it to follow the Universal Education principles that Lama Yeshe laid down, integrating the best of Western education with the essence of the Tibetan system. In this way Western society will benefit, and so will Tibetan. Of course,' she added, 'everything should be developed with His Holiness the Dalai Lama being the principal guide.'

It was a dazzling scheme and had some merit, but I wondered how Maria would find the teachers, let alone the finance, for such an ambitious plan. Few high lamas would be prepared to go against Lama Zopa Rinpoche's directive, as Maria herself had discovered when she had approached one or two to ask them to come to Bubion now to teach Lama Osel. In fact, Lama Zopa's wisdom was not to be tossed aside lightly. From the bottom of his heart he believed that Sera was the best place for Lama Osel to be, and who could dare contradict that?

Wondering where Lama Osel was now heading, I left Bubion. My last glimpse of the Spanish tulku was in the garden, where he was playing with his normal gusto. He was now 'free' and leading the life of an ordinary child, but I could sense something heavy and sad in him. At this stage of his life Tenzin Osel Rinpoche was a child caught between two cultures. It was a heartrending sight.

I returned to London with a heavy heart, confused by the conflicting interests that were now being played out within the context of Osel's life. Once more I wondered if the experiment of transplanting Eastern spiritual masters into Western soil would work. But above all my heart went out to the small Spanish boy whose destiny it was to be the spearhead of such a movement.

Then suddenly the crisis was over. A few weeks later Osel visited his father in London and decided of his own free will to leave Bubion and go to Kopan, the hill in the middle of the Kathmandu valley where it had all started. He wanted to resume his life as a monk. There, according to onlookers, he visibly relaxed for the first time in months. His harrowed expression and obvious unhappiness dissipated. 'It was as though he had refound where he belonged. It was as if he had come home to his real family,' commented one observer. He spent hours every morning with Lama Zopa in his room, where the constant peals of laughter coming from behind the closed door raised everybody's spirits. The young boy and the now middle-aged guru had re-established their indefinably close bond.

Lama Osel had clearly come to some fundamental decision about his life. He had chosen. For a short time he had tasted the ordinary life of a child, and then had voluntarily rejected it. His decision was made absolutely clear when a meeting was called between Maria, Paco and the heads of the FPMT, to discuss future plans for Lama Osel.

Although he was only nine, he took total control. Before the meeting started he actually rehearsed with some of the FPMT leaders how it should progress. 'He was just like Lama

Yeshe, taking the reins, directing the whole proceedings. He actually said, "I am the boss." It was impressive,' said one participant. In short, Lama Osel declared that he was going back to Sera, but on certain conditions – that his father Paco and his younger brother Kunkyen would go with him. He made stipulations about the new Western teacher he was to have (Norma Quesada-Wolf had left in the meantime) and the type of cook he wanted. He was clear, straightforward and full of authority. Much to her consternation, he even crushed Maria's arguments about him being better off in Bubion. 'He spoke strongly to her, but because he spoke the truth, she accepted what he said,' added the onlooker.

So now Lama Osel is back in Sera with his father as his attendant and his brother as his companion – as he requested. Kunkyen has subsequently become a monk, eagerly taking robes soon after he arrived, thereby beginning to fulfil the prediction that he too is a special child. He is settled and happy, and diligently getting on with his studies. Maybe his new-found acceptance has come about because he has people around him who he knows love him for who he is, rather than for what he represents. Maybe it is due to the fact that he independently chose the direction of his own life. Maybe he had discovered for himself how disenchanting 'ordinary' life can be. Or maybe Osel managed to resolve something very fundamental within. Perhaps it was a hurdle that all tulkus had to confront at some point in their lives.

I recalled reading about a similar crisis that the young Chogyam Trungpa, the brilliant and controversial meditation master, had gone through. In his book *Journey Without Goal* he described the misery he went through as a tulku in Tibet, and its resolution:

In my education I was constantly criticized. If I leaned back I was criticized and told that I should sit up. Every time I did something right I was criticized even more heavily. I was cut down constantly by my tutor. He slept in the corridor outside my door so I could not even get out. He was always there, always watching me . . .

I had been brought up strictly since infancy, from the age of eighteen months, so that I had no other reference point such as the idea of freedom or being loose. I had no idea what it was like to be an ordinary child playing in the dirt or playing with toys or chewing on rusted metal or whatever. Since I did not have any other reference point I thought that was just the way the world was. I felt somewhat at home but at the same time I felt extraordinarily hassled and claustrophobic.

Then, very interestingly, I stopped struggling with the authorities, so to speak, and began to develop. I just went on and on and on. At that point my tutor seemed to become afraid of me; he began to say less. And my teachers began to teach me less because I was asking them too many questions . . . Something was actually working. Something was finally beginning to click. The discipline had become part of my system.

Even the Dalai Lama, who has spoken openly about the strictness and isolation he experienced as a child in the thousand-roomed Potala Palace in Lhasa, has conceded that in retrospect the discipline has held him in good stead.

At this point in his life Lama Osel seems to have found himself. He has settled back into his house at Sera with its garden and ever-growing menagerie of pets: he now has two dogs, a rabbit and a deer. Having his brother and father with him has given him a stability that was obviously lacking before. His emotional environment is more important to him than anyone realized: he was missing the presence of a real friend.

He has even settled down to his studies with his gen-la, who has modified the traditional approach slightly to include more explanation and commentary, and inspirational stories of great masters and saints, which Osel enjoys. The new Western teacher is about to start teaching from an English-based curriculum devised to take children all the way to university entrance level. He is keeping up his written and spoken Spanish, English and Tibetan, and is now teaching his brother English. Much to his delight, he has been given a computer with a wide range of educational software which allows him to learn aspects of language, mathematics, reading and deduction in the form of challenging games. East and West are, at last, finally merging.

Writing in the June 1994 edition of *Mandala* magazine, the FPMT's newsletter, Paco describes Osel's present state of mind and the flavour of their everyday life:

The period in Kopan was good for Lama. It allowed him to reintegrate himself into Sera, giving him time and space to meditate on it. But he had already decided to return when we were in London.

Lama seems happy in Sera monastery. In the company of his brother Kunkyen, Lama manifests the part of him that most needs to be understood, being a child.

On 25 March 1994, an Italian television crew visited us. They were doing a piece on Ganchen Rinpoche. They interviewed Lama with the usual questions: did he remember his past life? He said he remembered nothing. Did he feel like a Lama or a child? He said like a child. Did he understand all the things they were teaching him? He said some of it. What is his schedule? He answered at length, giving the full picture, class by class. Would he like to live in a family? He said yes, that he already lived in a family at Sera.

Lama Osel has at last come home. I was interested to note, however, that he was now following the stock response of all rinpoches when asked about their memories of past lives – denial. I had once asked Lama Zopa what he remembered of his past life, and he had replied, 'Blackness.' The Dalai Lama similarly replied that he remembered 'very little'. Self-aggrandizement is never a hallmark of true spiritual attainment. Once, however, the Dalai Lama almost gave the game away when he remarked, 'Among some people I know, when a more subtle level of consciousness is produced in meditation, they are clearly able to remember seven hundred, eight hundred, a thousand years back.'

What of the future? According to Lama Zopa's vision, Lama Osel will stay at Sera at least until he is thirteen. And then his Western education will begin in earnest, grounding him in the principles of modern science, psychology and the latest discoveries of our age. As such, he is being groomed to become a unique receptacle of disparate systems: the most esoteric mysteries of the East, together with the latest thrusts of Western thought. What he will do with these two converging but different streams of thought it is too early to judge, but the plan and the aspiration are enormous. In Lama Osel it is hoped that East and West will come together and forge a new dynamic, a new venture for humankind.

It was towards this goal that Lama Yeshe's life had been directed. Lama Yeshe, that incomparable Tibetan, had boldly abandoned the traditional methods of transmitting the holy dharma to find a different way in which to reach the Western psyche. How we had all responded! This was the lama who had used hippie language to get his message across. ('Buddhism is not about blissing out – Buddhism is facing reality!'); who had visited Christian monasteries and befriended Christian priests to learn about the West's predominant religion; who had disappeared alone to the Australian beach for three days to learn about beach culture, and who had abandoned his robes for a pair of shorts, a T-shirt and a baseball cap so that he could mingle with the people undetected; who had gone to the Gay Parade and Disneyland; who had used every pore of his being to get his message of love and wisdom across. Will Lama Osel take up where he left off? Will he fill us with inspiration and show us a new way of looking at life, like Lama Yeshe did?

When I look at Lama Osel I see so many similarities: the innate kindness; the almost unbearable caring he has for the suffering of humans and animals alike; the extrovert personality; the love of flowers, cooking, cars, even hats; his quickness; and, the most important quality of all, his profound, original mind. My greatest fear that this child would be conditioned to play a role has been thoroughly trounced by his own magnificent independent spirit. It is now proven beyond all doubt that no one will ever be able to make Lama Osel do what he does not want to do, or to be who he does not want to be.

We wonder what that way will be. He is being groomed, like any heir, to take over the helm of a large kingdom. In Lama Osel's case, his dominion is global. The organization that Lama Yeshe set in motion, his 'international family', the FPMT, has steadily grown since his death in 1984 and now comprises some sixty-seven different enterprises including centres in cities, country retreat centres, monasteries, nunneries, a publishing company, hospices, homes for the destitute, a leprosy project and an ambitious plan to build a sixty-foot statue of Maitreya, the Buddha to come, in Bodhgaya, the place where the Buddha attained Enlightenment. Being responsible for such a vast organization, and its many problems and projects, is an awesome prospect. Lama Zopa has hinted that Lama Osel might begin to take the reins when he is thirteen.

There are those who fervently hope that he will. Those who have devoted their lives to establishing and running the various centres and projects that Lama Yeshe started (with all the devotion and self-sacrifice that that has entailed) are waiting for the inrush of energy and new life that Lama Osel will inject into their endeavours. Likewise, those first Westerners who were inspired by Lama Yeshe to shave their heads and put on the maroon and yellow robes expect Osel to become a great lama following in his predecessor's footsteps. For many, anything less than Lama Osel becoming a teacher in the Gelugpa Tibetan tradition will mean that he has failed.

Others feel that Osel does not have to be in monk's clothing to fulfil his destiny as a spiritual leader. They can envisage him going in a different direction, blazing a trail into a world other than that of Tibetan Buddhism. He came this time as a Westerner, they argue, and will use his special wisdom and compassion in a new format. Keeping to his robes and teaching as a lama from Tibet would be merely going backwards. One devoted Lama Yeshe disciple can see Lama Osel as a chat show host. 'Well, look at Oprah Winfrey. She reaches a huge audience around the world. If you want to get your message across, that's the way to do it,' she says. Another argues, 'If he had wanted to be a Tibetan following the Tibetan path, he would have chosen a Tibetan mother.' As for Osel's own mother, Maria states quite clearly: 'I believe Lama Osel has come to be a universal teacher, not a Tibetan geshe.'

Nothing is certain. Lama Zopa has made no secret of the fact that it is by no means assured that everything will be successful for Lama Osel, and that there are pitfalls and obstacles that we must constantly watch for. According to Buddhist philosophy, we might have the cause to have an eminent lama in our midst to teach and guide us, but the conditions we provide, the environment and our interactions with him are of equal importance. Everything is interdependent.

For myself I welcome Lama Osel's strong, sometimes way-ward energy. I am happy that he is a thoroughly Western child with a predilection for all the technological gadgetry of our times, and I secretly hope he is going to continue to be radical. For I have missed Lama Yeshe's nonconformist approach; his wide, ecumenical stance; his ability to cut through the complex structure of Tibetan Buddhism to deliver to us its essential message; his capacity to make Buddhism relevant and alive to us – the people of the West. Deep down, I hope that Lama Osel will find the means to put the precious ancient truths into a new language of the twenty-first century and to give meaning to this exciting, unpredictable world we live in.

The speculations go on. In the meantime I wait and watch with hope, excitement . . . and a little apprehension.

11

THE WHEEL CONTINUES TO TURN

My journey around reincarnation had taken me to many countries and brought me into contact with some of the most fascinating and illuminating people on earth today. The work they are doing, the revelations they are making, the challenges they are posing simply by being here are, I believe, pushing humankind to new boundaries of self-discovery and thought. It is an exciting time to be alive. Looking back over my travels, mental and physical, I can see some definite paths emerging in the landscape.

The new science launching out on its trajectory to explore the unknown realms of inner space, the most exciting dimension of all, is meeting a similar path coming from the East. Tibetan Buddhism with its own profound science of mind, gleaned through centuries of inner experience via meditation, has at last come out into the world, offering its treasure to us all. The moment is propitious, and the convergence promises to be fruitful indeed. There were a few individuals, visionaries of course, who saw it coming. H. G. Wells was one. He wrote: 'It is possible that in contact with modern science, and inspired by the spirit of history, the original teachings of Gotama (the Buddha), revived and purified, may yet play a large part in the direction of human destiny.' Another was Einstein, who spoke these prophetic words at Princeton Theological Seminary on 19 May 1939:

The religion of the future will be a cosmic religion. It should transcend a personal God and avoid dogma and theology. Covering both the natural and the spiritual, it should be based on a religious sense arising from the experience of all things, natural and spiritual, as a meaningful unity. Buddhism answers this description.

But, still, when I listen to the scientists standing at their lecture podiums arguing in their dry and intellectual way about the crucial issue of who we are, what makes us tick, and whether the brain is the same as the mind, I remember that in the East yogis are simply getting on with it. The great adepts are providing the visible and tangible evidence that they can, and do, control death. And that, after all, is the ultimate response to what consciousness is. While we are talking, they are sitting down in the meditation posture and actually demonstrating that human beings can die with full control over their mind – and apparently be reborn according to our own volition as well. It is an astonishing feat. Their accomplishment remains the biggest challenge to Western thinkers. I wonder if the scientists will take it up. The vital difference between the scientists and the yogis, however, is that the former are operating from their heads, while the latter are operating from their hearts. The question now is: will head and heart meet?

Then I see another path forming – that made by the coming of the Western tulkus and the spread of Buddhism to the West. The tulkus – those beings who, we are told, have voluntarily taken rebirth in order to show us the way – are now appearing in our midst as beacons to illuminate the possibility of what human beings can achieve. With their two wings of wisdom and compassion, expressing the head and the heart, they fly straight to the core of the matter. For myself their living presence is nothing less than inspirational – for only the tulkus and the message of Buddhism make any sense of the notion of coming back again and again to this life.

For when I look back on the mass of stories I have gathered from Westerners about their experiences of rebirth, one thing is clear: that going round and round in an endless cycle of birth and death with its myriad forms of pain and anguish is not only exhausting but ultimately tedious. It is what the Buddha said.

While some may be dazzled and hugely relieved by the fact that death does not end in oblivion, finally you have to ask, 'So what?' What *is* the point of this perpetual journeying through lifetime after lifetime? The Western findings might provide critical evidence that such a thing as rebirth exists, but it has not, so far, proffered any rationale behind the phenomenon.

Buddhism does. With its extensive study of the workings of consciousness and the logic of the law of cause and effect, Buddhism at least sets up a coherent argument for how we happen to be here, why we have the sorts of lives we have, and what will happen to us when we die. Whether we believe them or not is another matter. These are the biggest questions of all – ones to which we are beginning to demand answers. And so I watch with gathering interest the fragile path that Buddhism is now forging towards the West. I know that the dharma, the way the Buddha taught, doesn't actually belong anywhere. It is like truth floating on an ocean – it simply moves where the current of the times takes it and adapts itself to the colour and flavour of the country in which it finds itself. Now it is floating in our direction; it is our turn. I see no Western Buddhism yet, for it has to be taken in, digested and reformed according to our psyches. That will take many years. The Western tulkus are essential parts of that process, to help it on its way.

As to the Buddha's answer to why we keep on being reborn, he replied that the only point of it all was to learn how to stop. When disenchantment with continuous travelling sets in, when the fascination with our mind dramas, both tragic and comic, ceases, then we yearn for peace. That's when we begin our final journey to discover our true nature and the absolute reality of all things.

And yet while it is eventually our destiny to get off the circle of confused and suffering existence, I suspect the journey goes on and the wheel continues to turn.

GLOSSARY

Bodhicitta Altruistic attitude that wishes to release all beings from their suffering.

Bodhisattva A person intent upon reaching Enlightenment for the sole purpose of liberating others.

Buddha A fully-awakened being; one who has reached Enlightened, the totally omniscient mind together with absolute compassion.

Chenrezig (Sanskrit Avalokitshvara) A deity expressing the compassionate nature of the Buddha.

Dakini Female Enlightened being. Often called a 'sky-dancer'.

Dharma Spiritual teachings; the Buddha's way; the 'path'.

Emptiness (Sanskrit Shunyata) Refutation of the apparent independent self-existence of all phenomena; voidness.

Gelugpa One of the four sects of Tibetan Buddhism, also known as the Yellow Hat sect, founded by 14th-century reformer Je Tsong Khapá.

Geshe Monastic degree equivalent to a doctor of divinity.

Gompa Temple; shrine room.

Heruka Male deity of highest yoga tantra.

Lam Rim Teachings composed by Tsong Khapá delineating the step-by-step path to Enlightenment.

Mandala A representation of the mansion or universe of a Buddha.

Mantra Sacred words of power, usually Sanskrit.

Mudra Hand gesture symbolising Enlightened quality.

Nirvana State beyond sorrow and suffering – freedom from karma.

Osel 'Clear light' – the primordial mind of Enlightenment.

Rinpoche A recognised reincarnate lama. One who has voluntarily been reborn to help lead others to Enlightenment.
Stupa Monument whose dimensions represent the holy mind, body and speech of a Buddha.
Tantra Advanced teachings of Tibetan Buddhism practised only after initiation.
Tulku See Rinpoche.
Zopa 'Patience'.